Natalie and Romaine

Diana Souhami

Quercus

First published in Great Britain in 2004 by Weidenfeld & Nicolson
under the title *Wild Girls*

This edition published in 2013 by

Quercus
55 Baker Street
Seventh Floor, South Block
London
W1U 8EW

A CIP catalogue record for this book is available
from the British Library

ISBN PB 978 1 78087 882 9
ISBN EBOOK 978 1 78087 883 6

10 9 8 7 6 5 4 3 2 1

Text designed and typeset by Ellipsis Digital, Glasgow
Printed and bound in Great Britain by Clays Ltd, St Ives plc

Contents

To Roley 1986–2003
may the hedgerows of heaven smell of rabbits
And to Anne

A Personal Note

Wild Girls was the title of this book when it was first published in 2004. I am glad it is reissued as *Natalie and Romaine*. I was uneasy with *Wild Girls* and its cover picture of a woman's torso laced into a corset. The revised title is more appropriate to Natalie Barney and Romaine Brooks, their long relationship and cultured, creative lives in Paris, the city of light, in the first half of the twentieth century. It fits with other dual biographies of mine also being reissued: *Gertrude and Alice*, *Greta and Cecil*, and *Mrs Keppel and Her Daughter*.

Natalie and Romaine, both American, rich, and grandly lesbian, met in Paris in 1915 when they were in their forties. Their characters – Natalie's *joie de vivre* and Romaine's Gothic gloom – their abiding love which lasted more than fifty years, and their other, less enduring relationships, are the focus of this book.

Despite declared commitment to each other they did not live together, except for an enforced six months during the Second World War. Natalie, in particular, had no intention of fidelity. For her, 'living was the first of all the arts', and living meant seduction and lots of sex. She liked lavish display and theatricality and wanted not to bind love to rules, particularly to the rule of exclusivity. She inspired and befriended her lovers and broke their hearts. She divided her amours into liaisons, demi-liaisons, and adventures, and called her nature *fidéle/infidéle.*

I dwell only on her liaisons, before and during her relationship with Romaine. Her demi-liaisons and adventures were many. The acerbic view of Alice B. Toklas (Gertrude Stein's wife and muse),[1] was that Natalie picked up casual lovers in the toilets of Paris department stores.

Paris was essential to Natalie. She aspired to make it 'the sapphic centre of the western world'. She took as a model Sappho and the idea of a community of women who were artists and lovers.[2] At Natalie's 'dazzling' Friday afternoon salons, in her Grecian Temple of Friendship in the walled garden of her home in rue Jacob in the sixth *arrondissement*, 'one met lesbians,' Sylvia Beach said.[3] 'Paris ones, and those only passing through town . . . ladies with high collars and monocles, though Miss Barney herself was so feminine.'

Romaine, for her part, had no interest in salon life. She 'remained Romaine', as she put it, and resisted a sense of belonging to a place or time. To protect her artistic soul she kept aloof from relationships and trusted no one but Natalie, who perhaps was in love

---

1 Gertrude Stein (1874–1946) and Alice Babette Toklas (1877–1967) were at the heart of Paris cultural life between the two world wars. They first met on Sunday 8 September 1907. From that day on they were together until Gertrude's death on Saturday 27 July, thirty-nine years later.

2 Sappho (seventh century BC) was the first woman poet. Plato called her the tenth muse. She lived on the Greek islands of Lesbos and Leucas, and her poems extolled her love for women. Only fragments of her verse survive.

3 Sylvia Beach (1887–1962) first opened her bookshop Shakespeare and Company in 1919 at 8 rue Dupuytren, then in 1922 moved to 12 rue de l'Odeon, opposite Le Maison des Amis des Livres, run by her partner, Adrienne Monnier. Sylvia Beach published and distributed James Joyce's *Ulysses* when it was banned in England and the US. She was interned by the Nazis in the Second World War.

with her unavailability. Romaine suffered Paris and sought tran-
quillity in Capri and Fiesole, and in her elegant studios, though
she never stayed anywhere long. Her prime interest was herself,
her portraits of herself, and those she painted of women lovers
and friends.

From the start my favoured title, though I was alone in wanting
it, was not *Wild Girls* or *Natalie and Romaine*: but *A Sapphic Idyll.*
That was the title used, in French, by one of Natalie's more flam-
boyant lovers, Liane de Pougy, courtesan to aristocrats and the
Prince of Wales, for her memoir of her own extravagant affair with
Natalie.

A sapphic idyll: the lives, love affairs and artistic contribution
of lesbians in Paris between the two world wars, form the wider
context of this book, beyond the relationship between Natalie and
Romaine. In Britain, up until 1959, censorship deemed lesbianism
inadmissible. Radclyffe Hall's anodyne novel *The Well of Loneliness* was given a shaming trial and burned as obscene in 1928. A
pall of silence followed for decades. Creative lesbians from Britain
and America escaped repression and the 'rigid protocol' of their
home towns, and headed to Paris and the freedom to express themselves according to their own rules. The modernist revolution
would not have happened without their contribution: Sylvia Beach
who published *Ulysses*; Gertrude Stein's innovative prose and cham-
pioning of the new in art and literature; Bryher – Winifred Ellerman
– who financed Shakespeare and Company, the Egoist Press and
the Contact Publishing Company, which published, often for the
first time, Ernest Hemingway, Gertrude Stein, Djuna Barnes, Mina
Loy, James Joyce; Bryher's lover, the imagist poet Hilda Doolittle;
Dolly Wilde – Oscar's niece; Djuna Barnes who wrote the satirical

Ladies Almanack, then *Nightwood* about her relationship with the silverpoint artist Thelma Wood; Radclyffe Hall; the poet Renée Vivien; Colette; the dancer Ida Rubinstein . . .

The list is long. Natalie once drew a dense maze of the written names of those who visited her Temple of Friendship with herself threading through, uniting them all. Many had their portraits painted by Romaine. Visiting Romaine's studio, the writer Truman Capote, seeing these portraits, described it as 'the all-time ultimate gallery of famous dykes'. They formed, he said, 'an international daisy chain'.

Natalie made real her sapphic dream. But there was irony in my intended title. Her idyll cast long shadows. Dolly Wilde died alone in a rented room of alcohol and drug addiction when she was forty. Renée Vivien died of anorexia when she was thirty-one weighing under six stone. Romaine, haunted by her own disturbed childhood, famously wrote, 'My dead mother stands between me and life.'

I chose an unorthodox structure in the hope it was appropriate to these unconventional women who were innovative in their work and lives. The many odd-ball footnotes were meant as a mild spoof of biography's claims to authority and objectivity. The quasi-auto-biographical snippets that interpolate the narrative of Natalie's exuberant affairs, and self-sacrificing relationship to Romaine, were to show allegiance to the subject matter of the book, but also to undercut Natalie's Temple of Friendship and privilege. These discursions alight momentarily on a few unmoneyed realities of more ordinary lesbian life in 21st century London. In this reissue I have left them unedited, though ten years on, different random snapshots might come to mind: facebook messages perhaps, or a couple of tweets; the Iranian student living with her girlfriend in London,

4

but unable to tell her parents back home for fear of being stoned to death; the woman high on the balcony of a tower block who each morning waves goodbye with a red scarf as her lover makes her way down the station steps.

In the years between first publication and this reissue times have changed and I am older. But the personal remains political. As Natalie, 'the Amazon', the 'wild girl from Cincinnati' who each morning rode bareback in the Bois de Boulogne, hosted 'dazzling Fridays' and loved aphorisms put it: 'I am a lesbian. One need not hide it, nor boast of it, though being other than normal is a perilous advantage.' Or, 'People call it unnatural. All I can say is, it's always come naturally to me.' Or, 'Be one of life's equals.'

D. S.
2013

BEFORE ROMAINE

Liane de Pougy

*'I have watched women pass by, lit up by their
jewellery, like a city at night.'*

Liane de Pougy began each day with an enema. It kept her skin
clear and her breath sweet, particulars that mattered in her profession. A servant administered it with a syringe and it took a minute
or two to work. It was a custom copied from Madame Rhomés,
Liane's mother's great-aunt, who even at ninety had a complexion
like lilies and roses.

Liane took her name from a favoured client, the Comte de
Pougy. Titles and the ways of the aristocracy impressed her, especially when allied to money. She viewed lax manners as a moral
lapse and was outraged when the poet Max Jacob[1] was late for
lunch: her asparagus soup had thickened and the risotto had
congealed.

She was complimented on the splendour of her jewellery, her fine

---

[1] Max Jacob (1876–1944), writer, poet, painter. In 1909 he had two visions of Jesus
Christ, after which, though born a Jew, he converted to Catholicism. He spent much
time meditating and praying in the Benedictine Abbey at Saint-Benoit-sur-Loire. He
died in a concentration camp in Drancy.

carriages and inexhaustible wardrobe, her town house in Paris, and lesser houses in Brittany and St Germain. In her prime she employed four Arab servants: a cook, a lady's maid, a scrubber and a house-keeper and she served peacock foie gras with the champagne.

She spent her mornings in bed. Her dressmaker or milliner might call at midday. On a single visit from Paul Poiret[2] she chose fifteen of his designs: a dress in black wool with white embroidery and fringes, another in black silk with organdie flounces, silver tassels and a violet bow, a coat in black and gold with sable collar and cuffs.

Whatever she wore she flirted with it – the moue of her lips against the mesh of a veil, the lifting of her skirt to entice with a leg, the splaying of fingers over the fur at her throat. Such attention to detail and seductive gesture put her above the commonplace. She was of the *belle époque,* the *demi-monde,*[3] a courtesan not a tart.

She was as voracious for jewels as for clothes. Paris society columns of the 1890s made many a reference to 'our beautiful Liane de Pougy', radiant in dazzling white ermine and adorned with pearls. In Kursk in Russia, one of her clients, Count Vladimir Miatleff, 'a poet and a madman, impotent and a masochist, of the highest nobility, more ancient than the Romanoffs', summoned a Paris jeweller Jacques Goudstikker to his estate so that Liane might choose a jewel as payment. Goudstikker showed her a ruby and diamond tiara, an emerald necklace, a diamond chain, a parure[4] of turquoises and diamonds. Liane could not decide and asked for Miatleff's help. He told her to take the lot. 'I took the lot. He was a great nobleman.'

---

2 Paul Poiret (1879–1944) trained at the House of Worth then set up on his own in 1903. He acted, too. In 1926 he appeared with Colette in *La Vagabonde* in Monte Carlo.

3 A phrase coined by Alexandre Dumas the younger (1824–95), author of *La Dame aux Camélias* (1848).

4 A set of jewels to be worn together.

She described herself as vain but not a fool. She cultivated a conversational interest in painting, books and poetry, but avoided depth which she considered dull. Her clients did not pay her to stretch their intellects. She preferred café-concerts and popular songs to Shakespeare or Wagner, and made minor appearances in the chorus of the Folies-Bergère in Paris, in pantomime in St Petersburg and in cabaret clubs in Rome and on the French Riviera.

She was a conscientious bookkeeper, spent five thousand francs without a thought but was careful over five, and said she made all the minor decisions of her life, like marriage, or buying a house, by tossing a coin.

She was born Anne-Marie Chassaigne in 1870 in the Breton city of Rennes. Her mother, a tired-looking woman with large ears, while giving birth hallucinated that St Anne d'Auray, patron saint of the Bretons, prophesied that the child was destined for sainthood. Anne-Marie, even after her metamorphosis into Liane de Pougy, took the prediction seriously. An over-large pearl-encrusted crucifix often bumped below her secular beads.

She had no pleasant memories of childhood as Anne-Marie. To quell curiosity about breasts and vaginas her mother made her wear a chemise in the bath and sold pieces of household furniture to pay for her board at the Convent of the Sacred Heart. Anne-Marie abhorred such primness and scrimping and the sight of her father's worn-out coat and shoes. She became a compulsive pilferer and schemed to escape, to be free and to better herself.

At sixteen she ran away with a sailor, Armand Pourpe. They took lodgings in rue Dragon in Marseilles and their only possession of value was a rosewood piano. They got married when she became pregnant with her son, Marco. She would have preferred the baby to have been a girl 'because of the dresses and the curly hair' and was, she said, a terrible mother. 'My son was like a living doll given to a little girl.'[5]

'Events' and her husband's bookkeeping drove her, in 1889, into the arms of the Marquis Charles de MacMahon to the agitation of his wife. He was her fourth lover in three years of marriage. The others were a naval lieutenant, a professional gambler, and the Marquis de Portes. When her husband, goaded by such infidelity, shot at her with a revolver and wounded her in the wrist, she advertised the rosewood piano for sale. A young man came to view it, bought it for 400 francs, cash down, and within an hour Anne-Marie was on her way to Paris.

She set up as a courtesan with the Comtesse Valtesse de la Bigne, whose monumental bed was made of varnished bronze. The comtesse was the inspiration for Emile Zola's *Nana*, was painted by Edouard Manet, and her seductive success was commemorated in a stained-glass window depicting Napoleon III visiting her in her boudoir. She taught Anne-Marie the profession: money was its goal and life-blood so clients must be rich, she must conceal vulnerability or sentimentality, she must not fear publicity, reproach or blame, or voice principles, morals, or sectarian beliefs. She was to remember that her work put her 'outside of society and its pettiness'. 'Don't be sensitive,' Valtesse de la Bigne advised.

So Anne-Marie Chassaigne became Liane de Pougy and a shrewd businesswoman. Such kisses, caresses and spasms as she allowed were strictly in exchange for gold. 'What is your heart? – that thing

---

5 Marco Pourpe volunteered as an airman in the First World War. He was killed on 2 December 1914 near Villers-Bretteneux.

which beats for the pleasure you expect from me.' Aspects of her work were disgusting. Many of her clients were intolerably fat, contemptuous of women or unbecomingly peculiar. They paid for fantasy and sexual oddity unavailable at home. They did not ply her with jewels because they liked women, nor was she accommodating because she liked their little ways. Far from it. The essence of the contract was that she served those who could afford her. The organs of Albert, Prince of Wales[6] and Maurice de Rothschild[7] were royal and rich and more than paid the bills.

Her work at times was demanding: there was 'a very rich and very ugly Jew' whose manners she disliked; a 'silly Bonapartist' who instructed her to lie waiting for him in a transparent negligée on her polar bear rug, then straddled her and farted; a gambler who smoked fat cigars and paid for her to be exclusively available night and day in a bed at the Grand Hotel Monte Carlo; an unstable, 'so ugly' aristocrat, Frédéric de Madrazzo, 'too nervous, too excited', who soaked her sheets in sweat . . . But in payment for a stint she might receive 'a necklace of the white pearls I love worth one hundred thousand francs'. She accommodated her clients in a Louis XV bed, had more clothes than a bevy of maids could manage, slept in pale blue silk sheets hemmed with lace, and travelled from lord or prince to duke and count with quantities of expensive luggage. And when, on 13 May 1903, her five-row pearl necklace was stolen in rue de la Néva in Paris, her grief was brief. The client bought her another and a platinum ring stuck with diamonds.

---

6 Liane invited the prince to her debut at the Folies-Bergère: 'Deign to appear and applaud me and I am made.' He did and she was.

7 Le Baron Maurice de Rothschild. His waywardness and refusal to work in the family bank alienated him from his father, Edmond.

2

More Liane de Pougy

'I only know what I want.. And what I want,
would you want it?'

The Bois de Boulogne in 1899 was a pastoral setting for women of the carriage class in the mood to meet a perfect stranger. Open landaus, proceeding at a slow trot down the Passage des Acacias and the rue de Seine, 'gave one the leisure to exchange long looks and half-smiles in passing'. One such exchange took place on a spring day between Liane de Pougy and a young American woman with white-blonde hair and blue eyes.

Natalie Clifford Barney was out with an ersatz fiancé, Robert Cassatt of Pittsburgh.[1] She was twenty-three, in Paris with her mother, and studying Greek so as to read Sappho. She aspired, she said, 'to be a poet at all hours and above all a poet of life'.

The talked-of marriage was to appease Natalie's father, Albert, a man of fabulous wealth with sleeked hair and a waxed moustache. Albert minded about propriety and society. He suffered the

---

1 Robert Cassatt's family made their money in railroads. His aunt was the impressionist painter Mary Cassatt (1844–1926), admired by Degas.

independent spirits and artistic aspirations of his wife and elder
daughter. His dissatisfaction with them was at its stormiest when
he was drunk. 'I can't and won't submit to his whims as you do,'
Natalie wrote to her mother. 'It doesn't pay. I think I shall be very
polite and never answer him back, but have my own way when
it's reasonable, just the same.'

Having her own way meant her way with the ladies. As she saw
it, her sexuality was hers, not her father's. Her ambition was to
explore her own desires and be true to her own life. 'The first of
all arts should be the art of living.' In an autobiographical piece
she wrote of how, as a child at bath-time, 'the water that I made
shoot between my legs from the beak of a swan gave me the most
intense sensation.' It soon mattered that this sensation should ally
to art, life, and a Sapphic concept of loveliness. She divided her
amours into liaisons, demi-liaisons, and adventures, and called her
nature *fidèle/infidèle.*

After the swan came Ellen Goines, a cousin, who would flirt
and canoodle but no more. 'Nothing can move you and nothing
disturbs you,' Natalie complained of her. More compliant was
Evalina Palmer, famed for her sea-green eyes, her acting skills, and
her 'fantastic tresses which reached to her ankles, shimmering with
the whole spectrum of reds'. 'A liaison followed,' Natalie wrote in
Souvenirs Indiscrets, 'where poetry, Plato and nakedness all had a
part in our Arcadian life . . . We knew the sensual delights of our
nakedness on the mossy riverbanks.'

Aged eighteen, Natalie found more sensual delights on a grand
tour of Europe, chaperoned by Miss Ely of Miss Ely's School for
Girls in Maine. On a Norwegian steamship she met Mrs Leonora
Howland, a violinist to whom she gave a heart-shaped diamond

brooch. Their love lasted from Trondheim to Paris. 'Only those to whom sensations seem more direct through another are lovers,' Natalie wrote.

In Paris two years later came Carmen Rossi, principal model at the Académie Carmen, where Natalie's mother, Alice, had enrolled in James McNeill Whistler's[2] course in oil painting for lady art students. Natalie and her mother were in smart lodgings at the nearby Villa des Dames. In the mornings, under Whistler's instruction, Alice Barney painted Carmen gazing into a handglass, or draped in a floral Spanish shawl. In the afternoons Natalie had sex with Carmen. She pledged undying love to her, sent her letters and flowers, wrote poems about her, and went with her to the fair at Neuilly. 'I have a lover,' she wrote. 'There are women whose black eyes sparkle with energy. They make me feel so irredeemably blonde.'

Monogamy did not appeal. Throughout her life the next seduction lured. She did not court approval or disapproval and made no apology for her pursuit of love. On that spring day in 1899 in the Bois de Boulogne both she and Liane de Pougy knew well the implication of their long look and half-smile. Natalie described herself as 'captivated' by Liane's beauty. She did not conceal these feelings from Robert Cassatt. Her mother thought him naive and no match for her spirited daughter, but Natalie was frank with him: she desired women not men, and it would ever be so. Cassatt, unfazed, said he desired women too, so a marriage of such commonality might succeed. It would placate her father, secure for them both an enormous income, and not disturb society's expectations of acceptable relationship.

---

2 James McNeill Whistler (1834–1903), American portrait painter. Alice Barney did a pastel portrait of him in 1898. 'It is very amusingly done, dear lady,' he said.

He did, though, balk at her passion for Liane de Pougy, who was, he said, 'nothing but a courtesan', a high-class whore with an infamous reputation. Natalie was undeterred. 'I knew little of the *demi-monde*. I imagined that this woman was in danger. I thought I would find it easier to save her if I married my fiancé.'

She sent flowers and importunate letters until Liane allowed her an afternoon call. To show a courtly intention to charm and woo, Natalie arrived dressed as a prince, in a hired costume embroidered with pearls. Her liking for this regal disguise dated from when she met Oscar Wilde in the Long Beach Hotel, New York, in 1882 when she was six. Boys had pelted her with preserved cherries, which stuck in her plaits. She ran along the hotel lobby, crying, and Wilde scooped her up and calmed her with his story *The Happy Prince,* whose heart breaks for the love of a swallow. He published it in 1888. It was a favourite for Natalie, and when, aged twelve, she had her portrait painted by Carolus-Duran,[3] she insisted on dressing as a prince.

A maid showed Natalie into a shadowy bedroom where a woman reclined on a chaise longue. Natalie knelt and proffered lilies and roses. Liane giggled from behind a curtain. 'I realised the figure in front of me was not my idol but a stand-in, Valtesse de la Bigne, and I got to my feet right away.'

Liane wafted out in diaphanous white. 'She said in her languid way, "Here I am."' Natalie was surprised by the strength of Liane's grip on her shoulder. Valtesse de la Bigne made her exit, but not before inviting Natalie to call on her, too, at her mansion on the corner of Boulevard Malesherbes and rue de la Terrasse.

---

3 Carolus-Duran, born Charles Auguste Émile Duran (1838–1917), taught John Singer Sargent.

Liane proposed a drive in the Bois. She put on lipstick and eye black, diamonds and pearls, sprayed herself with rose perfume and changed from the diaphanous white into a town suit her maid had laid out for her, with matching hat, gloves, and handbag. As they left she said to Natalie 'I already love your hair and the way your mind works.' 'And so,' said Natalie, 'we set off at a trot, drawn by two white horses toward the Path of Virtue.'

I

At the Ace Bar, Christine Shaw asked me what my star sign was and would I like to dance. She supposed I was a Pisces like Elizabeth Taylor and that the number seven would bring me luck. She lacked Liane de Pougy's strategic skills, financial acumen or shimmering self-importance. Christine was her given name, she was from Birmingham, not Rennes, her clothes were Carnaby Street, and she worked to pay the bills.

She treated me with sisterly protection and asked me what I was looking for. I went with her to Soho, waited in the shadows, and drank weak coffee from a polystyrene cup. Her routine was to strip until one-thirty, then serve a few clients before going home to her daughter.

I watched her wriggle out of leopard-patterned viscose, observed her fake tan, her ridged Caesarean scar. I felt I had chanced on an aunt in an unlocked bathroom and in confusion must say 'So sorry' and hurry out. The street was bright with neon. I took the night bus home.

3

'Sonnets de Femmes'

'Sensuality, wanting a religion, invented love.'

Natalie and Liane's carriage ride in the Bois de Boulogne began a lesbian display, a subversive fling. Natalie was a 'passionate rebel against a woman's lot'. She did not want to bind love to rules and said conventional people did this so no event would find them at a loss. Paris accommodated her overt rebellion; it would not have been tolerated in Washington.

The following morning she again called on Liane, with roses and cornflowers. Liane was in bed. Her pale blue silk sheets, she explained, were to honour the virgin saint to whom she had been consecrated at birth. They got to the point of the visit – kissing, nipping, delirium. Liane commended Natalie's hair 'like a moonbeam', her blue eyes and 'vicious white teeth'. They soaked in a perfumed bath, massaged each other and rolled about on the polar bear's fur.

In the evening they took a box to see Sarah Bernhardt as *Hamlet* at her own theatre.[1] Max Beerbohm called Bernhardt 'the Princess

---

1 Sarah Bernhardt (1844–1923), French actress. Her *Hamlet,* an adaptation commissioned by her from Marcel Schwob and Eugène Morand, ran for four hours.

of Denmark'.[2] Passers-by applauded Liane as she stepped from her carriage. Natalie dealt with the coachman and tickets.

Natalie compared Hamlet's passivity to the subjugation of women. Men, she said, made laws for their own benefit. It was her resolve to revise these laws to suit herself. Her rejection of male orthodoxies was bold, her secularism determined. There was no God, the Bible was man's fiction, an overprinted fable: '"God will punish you even to the third and fourth generation." Let's raise a glass of cool water to the health of the fifth generation.' Individuality was her ruling star: 'Might I be the one I am looking for?' and her indiscretion was an act of faith, her way of breaking silence, of being visible.

She pursued Liane out of desire but did not lose a feminist intention to save her from prostitution. Such salvation needed money made by men, for Liane had tastes more expensive than her own. The Barney trust dictated the terms of Natalie's inheritance: her father must die, or she must marry. A cursory ceremony with Robert Cassatt seemed the more manageable option. She persuaded him of the aesthetic of her exchange with Liane, 'especially the Caress and the Kiss as described by the poet Pierre Louÿs'.

Pierre Louÿs,[3] in 1894, fooled literary Paris by publishing what he said were his translations of an ancient Greek text of ninety-three songs by the poet Bilitis. In an accompanying essay he wrote of how a German archaeologist, Professor Heim, had broken into

---

2 Max Beerbohm (1872 1956), English caricaturist and writer of parodies, essays and one novel, *Zuleika Dobson*. He drew more than two thousand caricatures, many of them for *Punch*. In 1910 he moved to Rapallo in Italy.

3 Pierre Louÿs (1870–1925), French novelist and poet. In 1889 he founded the review *La Conque* – Swinburne, Maeterlinck and Marianné were among its contributors.

Bilitis' tomb on Cyprus and found her poems. It was all a hoax. Bilitis and her songs, dedicated to 'the young women of the future society', were an invention of Louÿs. In these songs, on the island of Lesbos, Sappho initiates Bilitis into same-sex love with the beautiful Mnasidika, whom she marries. In 'Desire' she sings, 'Never in my life had there been a kiss like that one.'

Cassatt agreed in writing to a 'chaste and intellectual' marriage. Natalie 'tested him to the point of martyrdom' but he kept his word. He was, though, doubtful about the family model she proposed. They were to adopt Liane to secure an inheritance for her. So Cassatt must not have sex with his wife because of her passion for their adopted daughter who was seven years older than she was and a famous courtesan. He wondered how the arrangement would benefit him, and feared he would be socially compromised. To placate him, Natalie took him to Maxim's in the rue Royale to help him pick up amenable women. She wore a black wig as disguise.

Nor was Liane convinced that this proxy parenting would assure her own security. She wanted to retire, but was not inclined frivolously to gamble away a lucrative career. Natalie underestimated her professionalism; Liane was a strategic operator who would not carelessly rescind control of her own income. Nor would she tell Natalie secrets of her trade: how to avoid pregnancy, sexual disease, violence. She said she loved Natalie but that love alone was not enough. She called her luminous and subtle, a ray of light that gilded everything it touched. 'There is no ugliness, no brutality, no dirtiness. I love to lie down beside her, be in her arms, fall asleep lulled by the thoughts she breathes in short sweet phrases. My Natalie is a gift from heaven.'

They had a stylish time together. Looking lovely mattered – long hair, frocks and jewels. They bought necklaces from Lalique[4] and rings inscribed with messages of love. They scorned the image of their friend Mathilde de Morny, who dressed in riding breeches and morning suits, cropped her hair, smoked cigars, and called herself Uncle Max.[5] '"Why try to resemble our enemies?" Natalie would murmur in her little nasal voice.'

They began but did not finish a one-act play about Sappho and the island of Lesbos. Both rejected the ethic of exclusive attachment: 'One is unfaithful to those one loves so that their charm will not become mere habit.' They used provocation and jealousy to enhance desire. One afternoon, Liane, in bed with Valtesse de la Bigne and 'refusing her nothing', hoped Natalie was suffering on the other side of the locked door. And for Natalie there was still Carmen, Eva Palmer and a legion of unencountered women.

Liane fantasised about 'a blessed little nook where we will love each other; words, caresses, light touches, all that is us,' but until it materialised work took her to Rome, Monte Carlo, Florence, and London. She was pleased to compose and receive letters about fires of desire and the woods of Lesbos. In turn, she sent billets-doux and telegrams from hotels and chateaux: 'My home is in you, moonbeam, spiritually in you, in the softness of your golden hair . . . little morbid languishing flower, come find me here.' But her pecuniary instincts were deep: 'I still need eight hundred thousand francs[6] before I can stop. Then I shall cable you: "Come take

---

4 René Lalique (1860–1945). At the Exposition of 1900 he showed jewellery as art. He used innovative materials and created ingenious forms.

5 Sophie-Mathilde-Adèle Denise de Morny, half-sister of Napoleon III and a lover of Colette's.

6 About £32,000.

me" . . . We'll really live. We'll dream, think, love, write books.'

In the summer of 1899 they went to England together. They stayed at an inn at Maidenhead and hired a boat on the Thames, then booked a suite at the Hotel Cecil in London. The papers wrote of Liane de Pougy's beauty, her white gown covered in pearls, her ermine coat and her hats wreathed with roses. But then Mr Barney arrived, suspicious of all that was rumoured of the company his daughter kept. He looked ill and thin, with bloodshot eyes and a mottled face. His tolerance of alcohol had diminished: one whisky and he was drunk.

He forbade Natalie to have anything more to do with Liane and took her to Dinard,[7] in Brittany, for a holiday with her mother and sister Laura. She went for long horse rides; read the poetry of Paul Verlaine,[8] Baudelaire[9] and Stéphane Mallarmé;[10] wrote symbolist verses in French about her lovers; and sent letters to Liane commending her androgynous beauty and skin like rose-tinted snow:

> Yesterday I rode twenty-eight kilometres looking for something of beauty, tired of my surroundings. I saw pipes, stones, old women, cows and sheep. One sheep refused to walk with the herd and was beaten. Am I like that sheep? Yes. I hoped the Breton women would look like you – another disappointment. But I see you, my beloved in the flowers of your country . . . I

7 A favourite resort of the aristocracy, the Nice of the North, the Emerald Coast.
8 Paul Verlaine (1844–96), of the Decadent School, like Baudelaire and Mallarmé. In 1867 he published a collection of erotic verses, *Friends*. He had an affair with Rimbaud whom he shot and wounded.
9 Charles Baudelaire (1821–67), author of *Les Fleurs du Mal*, who thought vice natural and virtue artificial.
10 Stéphane Mallarmé (1842–98), literary cubist, enemy of naturalism, author of *L'Aprés midi d'un faune*.

kiss and bite and breathe the perfume of these flowers . . . and you know what I am thinking about . . .

Liane knew. With her instinct to profit from sexual encounter, she began a memoir of their affair, *Idylle Sapphique*, a confession from the *demi-monde*. 'It's going well,' she wrote after twelve pages. 'I think you'll like it.' Natalie, apprehensive of the inclusion of her own letters, asked for their return. Liane refused. Natalie, she said, could recopy them and in future should keep duplicates.

In September Liane joined her for a month in Brittany. Natalie had found a secret love nest, a rustic villa at St-Énogat,[11] away from the disapproval of family or the requirements of clients. But Liane became disaffected: the Clifford Barneys snubbed her and Robert Cassatt wrote from Pittsburgh ending his erratic engagement. Natalie tried unsuccessfully to secure her inheritance without the proviso of marriage.

Then a letter came from la Valtesse accusing Liane of slacking and of evading her responsibilities and opportunities. Where was she? A charming young man of good family was offering 500,000 francs for her. It was not possible to run a business this way. Liane returned to Paris and wrote to Natalie of her intention to end the relationship. As Natalie could not extricate her from prostitution there was no point to her reproaches. '*Everyone* tells me to let you go, that we can have no future together.'

In Paris they could at least have a present together. But a friend of Mr Barney saw them there and wrote to him of 'things so repugnant that one has to pity the minds that have conceived them'.

---

11 A tiny fishing village near Dinard.

Natalie received a letter from her father demanding that she break with Liane or return to America. She replied with scorn:

> Ever since I remember you your one ambition for us was petty and worldly. Even religion was made a sort of social duty. One should go to church because it looked well, or because people would think it strange if we didn't. You must understand how petty, how ugly our whole bringing up was. You showed me at the age of twelve all that marriage means – the jealousness, the scum, the tyrannies – nothing was hidden from me. I was even made a witness when still a mere child of the atrocious and lamentable consequences an uncontrolled temper can have on a good and kindly woman . . . Seeing all this made me lose faith in you – respect for you. I no longer felt myself your daughter.

She did, though, give him false assurance that she would 'give up seeing the woman'. It stopped him coming to Paris to take her home.

Natalie and her mother moved to the Avenue Victor Hugo on the Right Bank. Their house had wood-panelled rooms and high windows. Alice had a salon and studio in it; she painted portraits in the mornings, entertained artists in the afternoons and was thankful for her husband's preference for the men's clubs of Washington. Natalie had a workroom where she edited thirty-five of her own love poems for publication. In a nine-page preface 'for those who never read them', she explained her daring in offering 'French verses to France' and her experiment with French poetic conventions of rhyme and verse: 'Nothing about me must surprise you. I am American.' She called the book *Quelques Portraits – Sonnets de*

Femmes. She did not explain the content, or that the poems were about and to her lovers. She wrote of breasts like lotus flowers on a tranquil pond, of hearts moaning like the sea, the scent of her lover's hair, her lovers' cries of joy like those of a newborn child.

Alice Barney's French was poor. She thought Natalie's friends made beautiful models, and did pastel portraits for the book, happy at professional collaboration with her daughter. It did not come into her thinking that these models were Natalie's lovers. The book was published in spring 1900 by Paul Ollendorff under the imprint *Société d'éditions Littéraires et artistiques.* A review 'Yankee Girl French Poet' by Henri du Bois[12] was printed in the *Washington Post* subtitled 'Sappho sings in Washington'.

Albert Barney read it, then instructed staff to prepare his summer residence at Bar Harbor in Maine for the imminent arrival of his family. Bar Harbor was a resort for the excessively wealthy. The Barney 'cottage', designed to resemble a Welsh castle, had twenty-six rooms and a castellated façade. Mr Barney went to Paris to collect his wife and wayward daughter, and to buy up and destroy the printer's plates and all available copies of *Sonnets de Femmes.*

On 7 July 1900 Natalie sailed with her parents to America on the *Saint Louis.* At Bar Harbor, Alice shut herself away to paint in her studio on the second floor of one of the castle's towers. She felt betrayed by Natalie and told her she had sinned, sullied the family name and made her mother a very unhappy woman. Because of her transgressions the family was ostracised, she said, more shunned than if they had killed someone. Natalie felt imprisoned. Albert drank.

---

12 Du Bois published Guy de Maupassant and Colette.

Late in the month he had a heart attack while playing golf. Illness spared him news of the publication of Liane de Pougy's *Idylle Sapphique,* although in Paris it was common knowledge that the Flossie Temple Bradford of the romance, who so fervently kissed the ankles, knees, legs and thighs of its author, was the rich wild girl from Cincinnati, the blonde-haired Natalie Clifford Barney who each morning galloped bareback in the Bois de Boulogne.

2

At lunch at the Palace Hotel, at the time of the Thorpe affair,[1] Nigel remarked 'I've nothing against homosexuals, I just don't want them running the country.'

'And neither do I,' said mother.

'That's rich,' I said, 'judging people by their sexual orientation, not their abilities.'

The conversation moved to other things. I ate my salmon en croûte. None of us wanted less than love. They feared that soon I too might stain the family name, with hired assassins on Bodmin Moor, and Rinka the great dane shot, if not the lesbian with whom they supposed me to be carrying on.

---

1 Jeremy Thorpe, leader of the Liberal Party, in court in 1978 was acquitted of hiring a hitman to kill his alleged former lover, a male model, Norman Scott. Rinka was Scott's dog.

4

The Princess Ghika

'In love there is no status quo.'

Natalie failed to rescue Liane from her profession, but in 1910 Liane rescued herself when she married Prince Georges Ghika, whose mother had a palace, vineyards and forests in Romania. Liane was forty-one and her prince was twenty-six. She visited him in a sanatorium when he was recovering from a breakdown. He had tried to kill himself after being jilted by an actress.

She obtained a dispensation for her past sins at the church of St Philippe du Roule in rue du Faubourg St Honoré, then on 8 June married the prince in the town hall. His mother viewed her daughter-in-law as a gold-digger, refused all contact with her, and as punishment restricted her son's allowance.

Natalie was not forgotten. Liane told her she was 'stupefied by tenderness' whenever they met. 'I love seeing her again, listening to her, watching her make her way through the world of her choice – easily the most charming of worlds.' But as Princess Ghika, she began to talk of the vice of lesbianism. She imposed a rule that caressing with women must now be only from the waist up. All from the waist down was reserved for Georges.

Georges's terrain had problems. On the surface the marriage seemed civilised: a house in St-Germain, investments in Central Mining and Royal Dutch Oil, roses pinned to Liane's mink coat, dinner parties with writers and composers: Jean Cocteau,[1] Salomon Reinach,[2] Max Jacob, Francis Poulenc,[3] first nights at the Ballets Russes, a cruise to Vancouver, holidays in Roscoff and at St Moritz . . . But Georges was not a straightforward prince. One day he admitted to fantasies. All the time he talked he pulled out hairs from above his left ear, while Liane sat on her bed playing patience and saying Oh and Ah. He revealed that he would like to bring prostitutes back and watch while they and Liane had sex. He wanted to solicit women and have very quick sex with them, 'because if I have to talk to a woman for twenty minutes I stop wanting her'. He would like to make a film about women having sex with women and men having sex with women having sex with women.

In 1926 he began an affair with a mutual friend of his and Liane's, the artist Manon Thiébaut, who carved wood and made linocuts. Small, slim and young, she was known as the Tiny One. Georges wanted to live à trois, and be with the Tiny One at nights. The maids need not know, he assured Liane, who filed for divorce

---

1 Jean Cocteau (1889–1963), French poet, writer, artist, filmmaker, 'on the look-out for every novelty', Natalie said. He wrote libretti for the Ballets Russes.

2 Salomon Reinach (1858–1932), German philologist, archaeologist and art historian. To Natalie's chagrin he deposited all Renée Vivien's papers in the Bibliothéque Nationale with an embargo on their being seen until January 2000.

3 Francis Poulenc (1899–1963), French composer, allied to cubism, influenced by Cocteau, and an admirer of Eric Satie. He played new works at Natalie's salons. In the twenties he wrote *Rhapsodie nègre* and the score for a Diaghilev ballet, *Les Biches,* about flirtatious girls.

saying he was murdering her and that God was her only consolation.

In 1946, towards the end of her life, Liane was received into the Order of St Dominic at Bois-Cerf in Lausanne as a tertiary lay sister. She looked pious in a wimple and was popular with the sisters and Mother Superior, but particularly with Bishop Herzog. Known as Sister Anne-Marie, she daily recited the Order's prayers, the rosary, and the gospel, and read tracts from Thomas à Kempis *The Imitation of Christ*. She also edited her confessional journal, *My Blue Notebooks* for publication. It was written in a quasi-revelatory style, which steered clear of any awkward disclosure of self. Within its pages she purveyed the sense that sanctity, like prostitution, lesbianism and marriage into the aristocracy, was one more deal made by a shrewd businesswoman – who had a flair for action and whose heart of gold was adept at totting the cost.

5

Lady Alice

*'What makes marriage a double defeat is that it works
on the lowest common denominator; neither of the
ill-assorted pair gets what they want.'*

In her parents' relationship Natalie saw a domineering, small-minded
man, a drunk and a social climber, who tried but failed to suppress
the free spirit and creative aspirations of his wife. She viewed it as
a tribute to her mother's will that she did not kowtow to him,
that she painted pictures, travelled independently, produced plays,
held salons, and set a standard for her daughters.

Natalie was scathing about alcohol, though she liked a glass of
port or vintage wine. Liquor, she said, brutalised the mind and
body. Drinking someone's health in it was a contradiction in terms.
'I loathe the enthusiasm, the writing, friendships and love affairs
that come from being drunk.'

Alice Barney inherited her fortune from the whisky that ruined
her husband. Her half-Jewish father, Samuel Pike, the son of New
York immigrants, left home when he was seventeen, moved rootlessly from state to state then settled in Cincinnati. When he was
twenty-two he married Ellen Miller, a judge's daughter. He set up
a distillery for 'Magnolia Whisky' and by the time Alice, his fourth

child, was born in 1857, he was a multimillionaire.

Money enabled him to be a patron of the arts. Pike's Opera House, modelled on La Scala in Milan,[1] and completed in 1859, turned Cincinnati into the cultural centre of the American Midwest. Alice, when young, went to all the productions there of her father's operas, ballets and plays. She saw him as a man of energy and imagination and her mother as a drudge: 'Nothing aroused her interest. I thought often of her life and vowed that mine should not grow into such an uneventful existence.'

But on the night of 22 March 1866, after a performance of *A Midsummer Night's Dream*, a huge cylinder of gas, used to light and heat the opera house, exploded. The fire it caused was seen for fifty miles. It destroyed the entire square: the Opera House, offices, and the printing works of the *Cincinnati Enquirer*. Pike was insured for $38,000, the damage cost over $1 million.

He moved his family to New York, to West 23rd Street, and worked to start again. He opened a new distillery, built, adjacent to his home, another opera house with a twenty-five-foot dome and a huge seating capacity – for 2,600 – and began a new business: The Iron Dike and Land Reclamation Company. Its aim was to acquire and drain 6,000 acres of Newark marshland, then sell the reclaimed land to the burgeoning railroad companies. Two years into the project, on 7 December 1872, Samuel Pike went to his office on Bridge Street, ate a dozen oysters for lunch at Delmonico's,[2] then died at his desk of a heart attack, aged fifty.

1 The Teatro alla Scala, built in 1776, seats 2,200 people. Pike's Opera House seated 3,000, was five storeys high, and adorned with Italianate murals and statues.

2 Delmonico's began as a pastry shop in the mid-1800s, then became New York's first restaurant.

Alice was seventeen. Her bereaved mother took her on a grand tour of Europe. Alice sketched impressions of Paris, Milan and Rome. In London, at the Langham Hotel, she met the explorer Henry Morton Stanley, back from an expedition to Africa to find the Protestant missionary and anti-slave campaigner, David Livingstone,[3] lost in Zanzibar. Stanley, after months of trekking, came face to face with him on 10 November 1871 under a mango tree in the village of Ujiji, on the east side of Lake Tanganyika. He greeted him with 'Dr Livingstone, I presume.'

Stanley, twice Alice's age, was eminent and impressive like her father. 'I had met Stanley . . . I had met the lion of London . . . It meant the lilt of life to me,' she wrote in an unpublished autobiographical piece. In his own diary Stanley wrote: 'I fear that if Miss Alice gives me as much encouragement as she has been giving me lately, I shall fall in love with her.' He gave her a ruby locket with his picture in it, took her to Windsor Castle, told her he loved her and would give up his explorer's life for her, and asked her mother for permission to marry.

Mrs Pike said Alice was still too young, but if he waited two years she would reconsider. Stanley agreed to wait, confiding to his diary, 'No man had ever to work harder than I have for a wife.' To fill the gap, he arranged a second expedition to Africa, to continue Livingstone's explorations in tracing the source of the Nile and the headwaters of the river Congo.

He went with the Pikes to New York to seek newspaper sponsors for this venture. On 12 July 1874, five days before he was to

---

3 David Livingstone (1813–73), explorer of North Africa, who discovered the Victoria Falls. He died two years after meeting Stanley. His heart was buried in Africa and the rest of him in Westminster Abbey.

leave, he and Alice signed a marriage pact: 'We solemnly pledge ourselves to be faithful to each other and to be married to one another on the return of Henry Morton Stanley from Africa. We call God to witness this our written pledge.'

On his last evening with her, Stanley wrote, 'She raised her lips in tempting proximity to mine and I kissed her on the lips, on her eyes, on her cheeks and her neck and she kissed me in return.'

He wrote to her daily while he travelled and named his sailing boat and an island in Lake Victoria 'Lady Alice' after her. But his letters illustrated the chasm between tribal Africa and affluent New York society. 'My present abode is a dark hut. Through chinks in the mud I can but faintly see these lines as I write. Outside naked men and women create a furious jangle and noise, bartering with my people for beads.'

Alice occasionally replied – breezy letters about plays and dances, and one that held a warning: 'I should hate to be poor, how envious I would be of rich people. Just think, if I had to give up my beautiful laces, silks and diamonds, my home and piano, horses and carriage.'

As with Liane de Pougy, money was crucial to Alice Pike and in turn to her daughter Natalie Barney. Money gave them confidence and freedom: to travel, to express themselves in poetry or painting, to pay for publication, to live for art and love. It absolved them from the squalor of envy and kept them ignorant of the hardship of life in a dark mud hut.

In spring 1875 on a visit to relatives in Dayton, Ohio, Alice was introduced to Albert Clifford Barney, a short man with 'a suave air of distinction'. His father was president of the Barney-Smith Car Works, the leading manufacturer of railway carriages for the

Midwest. Unlike Stanley, who had no money, the Barneys were very rich, though not as rich as the Pikes. Albert worked for the family firm and hated it.

Within weeks of their meeting he asked Alice to marry him. His proposal was so convoluted she did not at first realise he had made it. He took her awkward smile as acceptance then turned to her relatives for congratulation. It was lightly done. As well him as any other, she thought, but said neither yes nor no.

Stanley, trekking through Africa, was sustained by the thought of her. She tied his unread letters in ribbon and put them in a trunk. He reached Ujiji in May 1876 and was hugely disappointed to find no letters waiting from her. 'I had daily fed and lived on that hope . . . You may imagine how I felt when, after enquiring about letters, I was met with "There are none." . . . I soberly grieved and felt discouraged.' He did not know that his hope was four months married and four months pregnant.

Alice and Albert had honeymooned in New Orleans and Florida, then moved to a new house in Dayton, Ohio. As she unpacked her trunks, there among her gowns and wedding gifts were Stanley's letters. 'Albert's jaw tightened and his eyes became hard.' He ordered her to destroy them, and stood over her while she did so. As she watched them burn, the bleak realisation dawned that she had made a mistake. With it came loneliness and resentment at the curtailment of freedom. From her father she had learned to prize self-expression. Her husband wanted her to suppress what she felt.

'I could do nothing about it. I would go on, and be a "good wife", but my heart would never be in it. I would be living out a pretence . . . I had not been complete, never been a whole individual until that realization when my husband commanded me to destroy Stanley's letters.'

Stanley reached Zanzibar in November 1877. Among his waiting mail were clippings from the *New York Herald* about Alice's marriage and the birth of her first daughter, Natalie. He went into a deep depression. When he returned to England he received a letter from her:

> You must know, by this time, I have done what millions of women have done before me, not been true to my promise. No doubt before long you will think it a gain, for Stanley can easily find a wife who is all his heart could desire, to grace his high position and deservedly great name.
>
> If you can forgive me, tell me so. If not, do please remain silent. Destroy my letters as I have burnt all yours.

Two years later he sent her *Through the Dark Continent*, the story of his arduous journey. He enclosed a note:

> You spurred me on to achievement which I could never have accomplished without you. Your image was always before me, Lady Alice. It beckoned me, it commanded, sustained, and now it rewards me. Africa has been conquered and you, not I, have conquered it. With love in my heart I lay it at your feet, Lady Alice.

Albert Barney inherited when his father died in 1880. He moved his family to a lavish house in Cincinnati, hired a French governess for his daughters, indulged his passion for liveried carriages and elegant parties, and drank to excess at his club. He had wanted a society wife, moulded to his views. But only reluctantly did Alice ever do as she was told. She showed no temper, but no interest in anything he did. To her diaries she confided her criticisms of him: his eyes were set too near together, his ideas were prejudiced and narrow, he had no soul. Stanley, she wrote, was the only man she had loved.

She filled her life with pursuits that had nothing to do with Albert. Her disdain for him was communicated by her preference for the times when they were in different countries, her absorption in portrait painting, her desire to travel with her daughters but not with him. She was never confrontational. Natalie said that she never saw her mother cross. '"Live and let live" was her motto. She had great patience with difficult characters, ungenial though they might be. The desire to control other people was foreign to her. When anyone failed her she was more sorry for them than for herself.'

Albert Barney lived with his wife's pity, and thought her artistic aspirations affected. Worse, she liked Paris, the Left Bank, symbolism, and poetry. He complained that she was bankrupting him and he sought consolation in whisky and other women. He did not control his frustration and rage. Natalie believed that he cared for his family but that his love was thwarted. 'His affection for me was demonstrated with gifts and bruises: he would pull me back from the traffic with such vigor that I would have preferred the accident.'

She observed her parents' tensions and disappointments and generalised. Marriage, she concluded, was a farce, a grotesque joke, not an acceptable basis for relationship. She would not be governed by its tyranny, or walk into its trap. Were she to wed it would be as a ruse to gain her inheritance, no more. She was glad to be spared desire for any man and was, she said, 'naturally unnatural'.

Her first love was for her mother. From her she inherited an extravagant sense of self, a disdain for marriage, an enormous amount of money, and a habit of startling gesture and display. She called her love for her mother 'an absolute emotion':

> When she bent over my bed before she went out to a party, she seemed more beautiful than anything in my dreams. I would stay awake anxiously waiting her return, for whenever she was away I was afraid something terrible might happen to her.
>
> When she came home with my father, often very late at night, I would hear the rustling of her dress as she passed my bedroom. I would tiptoe barefoot toward the strip of light which shone under her door. I could not leave until she put out her lamp, though I trembled with cold and emotion.

3

Proust[1] when a boy, wheedled the maid to pass his mother a note, so that she might leave her dinner guests, come to his bedside, kiss him, and murmur goodnight.

And I, the door six-and-a-half inches wide, my plaits and arms beneath the sheet to save them from amputation, facing the fireplace, ignoring the wall where the Devil resided, listened as my mother prepared to meet her guests, and hoped she would think of me, and come and brush her lips against my cheek.

And even now, all superstition gone, lying uncovered in the warm night, the window open, shadows touching the walls, I am unnerved by the dark, as I hear your voice talking low on the phone in a downstairs room.

---

1 Marcel Proust (1871–1922). His masterwork was his 3,000-page novel *À la Recherche du Temps Perdu*. In his twenties he was a conspicuous Paris society figure: from 1907 he rarely emerged from a cork-lined room.

6

Renée Vivien

'Ever since God made Eve from Adam's rib
everything has been abnormal.'

A good scandal, Natalie said, was a way to get rid of nuisances. Mild disgrace gave liberation from society's prejudice. She met Renée Vivien in the winter of 1900. Renée was overly thin and subsisted on spoonfuls of rice, a little fruit, and quantities of alcohol and ether. She was tall, but slouched so as to appear less so, had a smooth complexion, heavy eyelids, a retroussé nose, a hand tremor and an engaging lisp. Her gestures were awkward, and she was always losing things – her gloves, money, scarves. She wore unsteady hats and long purple or black dresses. She translated the poetry of Sappho from Greek to French and in classical French wrote her own poetry about her love and scorn for women, and her longing to be dead.

She described her childhood as intolerable. Born Pauline Tarn in 1877, she was brought up in Paris and Paddington. Her mother was from Michigan and her father from Teesdale. Money came from her paternal grandfather who owned a chain of grocery stores in England. Her father drank, her parents quarrelled, and she said she was abused by carers. In Paris when she was thirteen she was passionate about an American friend, Violet Shiletto.[1] After three years they were separated: Pauline's father died of pneumonia after bathing in the sea near Étretat in Normandy, and her mother then moved with her to London.

Pauline shut herself in her room, wrote poems, read Victor Hugo, Byron, and Keats,[2] played Chopin piano sonatas and developed nervous headaches and fevers. When she was eighteen she tried to kill herself with chloroform. She confided her unhappiness in letters to Amédée Moullé, a middle-aged Parisian poet. 'If only I could live as I want to,' she wrote to him in May 1894: 'Love and marriage – it is only good for people who have nothing better to do, or who want some very harsh punishment.'

By the terms of her grandfather's will she stood to inherit when she married or reached twenty-one. Her mother resented her rebelliousness and potential wealth, suspected her of planning to run off with Moullé, and locked her in the house 'as in a gaol'. Pauline escaped through a window, pawned a brooch and took lodgings where she stayed five days. When servants found her she attempted to drown herself in the river Wandle.[3] Her mother tried to have her certified. Pauline accused her of wanting to cheat her of her inheritance, and the case was referred to the courts. Doctors judged her sane, made her a ward of court and assigned her a legal guardian. As soon as she was twenty-one, in 1898, she left for Paris.

1 Renée Vivien made the violet her symbol in memory of Violet Shiletto (1880–1901).

2 The Romantic Movement valued sensibility and feeling, over rationalism. Victor Hugo (1802–1945), French Romantic poet and novelist. Lord Byron (1788–1824) and John Keats (1795–1821), English Romantic poets.

3 Derived from the Saxon 'Wendleswurth', 'Wendel's settlement' and known today as Wandsworth, which is where the Wandle meets the Thames.

There, she broke from her inimical background and culture. She discarded the name Pauline Tarn, rejected the tyranny of her mother, the repressions of English society and any imperative to be happy. She desired to be reborn in French as Renée Vivien and to be free to write poems about lesbian love. Natalie said Paris was the only city where one could be who one pleased: 'Paris respects and encourages personality. Thought, food and love are a matter of personal taste and one's own business.'

In December 1900 Natalie was again in Paris with her mother, glad to escape the 'rigid protocol' of Washington parties, lunch-eons, and balls. Alice was painting portraits at the Académie Julian[4] in the rue du Dragon: Natalie was studying French classical verse with Charles Brun.[5] Riding in the Bois she was delighted to re-meet Violet Shiletto and her sister Mary. They had been childhood friends in Cincinnati. Violet told her of Renée and how she too wrote poetry in French.

The four arranged to go to a matinée. 'The butler announced the arrival of their landau and at the same time handed me an envelope on which I recognised Liane de Pougy's handwriting. She was travelling in Portugal.' Natalie thought Renée looked ordinary, paid scant attention to her or to the play, and at the back of the box read and reread Liane's letter. Liane was obliging a Prince, but her thoughts were of Natalie: 'The moon sulked and I thought of you moonbeam, of your fine, fine hair ... my little blue flower whose perfume intoxicated me oh so sweetly, you, my fair one,

---

4 Founded in 1862. A prestigious school for women artists who were banned from the École des Beaux-Arts until 1897.
5 A tall, thin, classical scholar and poet, author of *Chants d'ephèbe* and *Onyx et pastels*, He taught Natalie Greek and prosody.

my Flossie . . .' She said she remained enchanted with Natalie and took pleasure in returning to her from time to time.

After the play, in a carriage in the Bois, Violet invited Renée to recite one of her poems. Renée chose her favourite theme – her longing to be dead:

Lay down those funeral flowers on the white cover of my pillow.
Their scent disturbs me.
Lay them in my hands, on my heart, my forehead
Those pale wax-like flowers.

Next evening Natalie took her to the Palais de Glace[6] in the Champs Élysées. Renée was a superb skater. Natalie went back to Renée's apartment in rue Crevaux. It was filled with white lilies, in vases in corners and strewn on the bed. All the windows were closed and the curtains drawn. The effect was stifling.

Natalie left at dawn. A light frost covered the ground. It was, she said, 'a disquieting beginning in which two young women try to find themselves in a mismatched love affair'. Renée then bombarded her with flowers, jewels, and poems. Her love for Natalie, she wrote, was like the attraction of deep water, like standing at the edge of an abyss, like wedding-day chastity, like snow-pure passion. 'In you I find the incarnation of my deepest desire. You are more strange than my dream. I love you and I am already certain you will never love me. You are the suffering that makes happiness contemptible.'

---

6 In 1896 the artist Jules Cheret did a series of lithographs of the Palais de Glace, the women wrapped in furs, the men in high hats.

Natalie was concerned by the quality of this devotion. She would, she said, have preferred something simpler. Nor was all well in bed. Renée could not match Natalie's sexual ease. She was anxious and troubled. For her, love was an outpouring of poems. She valued writing more than living whereas Natalie's ambition 'was to make my life itself into a poem. I looked to life for the fullest expression of myself.'

Natalie regretted causing Renée despair, 'throwing her soul into disarray, I did not want it to be like that, rather that she should love me just enough to bring sunshine into her life.' But Renée was no sunshine girl, as the merest encounter made clear. She was melancholic, nihilistic, anorexic. Their relationship became one of bitter separations and exhilarated short-lived reconciliations. Natalie described it as defeated love. Renée was too complicated, too self-destructive. Nor could she cope with all Natalie's other lovers, ever in the wings: Liane de Pougy, Eva Palmer, Lucie Delarue-Mardrus . . .[7]

Then came Olive Custance. In 1901, *Opals*, her first volume of poems, was published in London. Many of the poems had a lesbian theme. Natalie, impressed, sent her an admiring letter and a copy of her own *Quelques Portraits – Sonnets de Femmes*. Olive responded with poetic invitation.

> For I would dance to make you smile, and sing
> Of those who with some sweet mad sin have played,
> And how Love walks with delicate feet afraid
> Twixt maid and maid.

---

7 Lucie Delarue-Mardrus (1880–1945), French poet and novelist, wife of Dr J.C. Mardrus, translator of the *Arabian Nights*. 'Natalie Barney,' she said, 'is that rare creature whom one does not meet twice in a lifetime.'

Natalie liked sweet mad sin and maid and maid. She invited Olive to Paris and suggested that with Renée they create a community of women poets, like Sappho on Lesbos, deriving inspiration from each other. Olive was enthusiastic and arrived, escorted by her mother, a neighbour Freddy Manners-Sutton,[8] and her aunt, Lady Anglesey.[9]

The launch of this Sapphic idyll had problems. Lady Anglesey was about to divorce her transvestite husband. Freddy Manners-Sutton fell for Natalie. Natalie was enchanted with Olive – her wonderful complexion, her vibrant poetry. Renée Vivien was morbidly jealous, and Olive was in love with 'Bosie', Lord Alfred Douglas.[10]

The Bosie connection fired Natalie's desire for Olive. Oscar Wilde, she said, had influenced her decision to be a writer. She was nineteen when she read of his relationship with Bosie, his trial and sentence to hard labour. She wrote to him in Reading Gaol, 'hoping to comfort him as he had comforted me, reminding him of his protection of me against the pursuit of little people. But did he ever receive my letter?'[11]

8 The Honourable Frederick Walpole Manners-Sutton, son and heir to the Viscount Canterbury. Renée called him a second-rate little cad.

9 Mary Livingstone King, the third wife of Henry Cyril Paget, 4th Marquess of Anglesey. She lived at Versailles and had a large collection of porcelain.

10 Lord Alfred Douglas (1870–1945), English poet. Oscar Wilde's consuming passion for him began in 1892. He described him as 'like a narcissus – so white and gold'.

11 In 1894 Bosie's father, John Sholto Douglas (1844–1900), the 9th Marquess of Queens-berry, wrote to him that if he again caught him with Wilde 'I will make a public scandal in a way you little dream of'. The following year Queensberry called Wilde a sodomite. Wilde sued for libel then withdrew from the case. He was arrested through on charges of gross indecency under the Criminal Law Amendment Act of 1885. Found guilty, he was sentenced to two years' hard labour, most of it served in Reading Gaol, where he wrote *De Profundis*. After his release in 1897 he lived in France, Italy, and Switzerland. He resumed his relationship with Bosie, and his wife Constance refused to see him. He died in a Paris hotel room on 30 November 1900.

Natalie called Olive 'Opale', spent evenings with her in her studio 'bathed in moonlight and poetry', said that to kiss her was like 'kissing the English countryside', and wrote love poems to her: 'Of all my cruel loves I love you most, and since I love you most – ah sweet, love me.' She said intense feeling inspired bad verse and that she hoped for the time when she would stop loving her, 'then perhaps I shall be able to sing of you as you deserve'.

Freddy Manners-Sutton persisted in declaring his love for Natalie, and ordered an engagement ring for her from a jeweller in the rue de la Paix. It was set with diamonds and had an enamel eye of a peacock at its centre to represent his coat of arms. When she told him she loved Opale he said it made no difference.

Opale pined for Bosie. They met in secret and wrote often. Bosie praised her for being beautiful, appreciative of his poetry, rich, and bisexual. Her father, an erstwhile colonel with the Grenadier Guards, could not be told of the romance. She was his only child, his heir: he was a magistrate, one of the Prince of Wales's set, and owner of Weston Old Hall near Norwich. All he knew or cared of Bosie was that he was Lord Queensberry's son, who had got himself into an appalling mess over the unspeakable Oscar Wilde.

Renée hated it all. She shut herself away, ate scraps, drank absinthe, and wrote antipathetic poetry about Natalie – her cold kisses and false laughter, her voice a treacherous tide, her arms like river reeds that choked and strangled as they embraced:

> The moon slanted over you, grazed you
> It showed you hideous beneath your beauty.
> I saw on your mouth the withered smile of an old whore.

She said she loathed everything English and in particular Opale. Natalie argued that Sappho welcomed women from all countries, and derived inspiration and desire from jealous lovers. Nothing and no one could separate her and Renée, she said. Renée thought the argument specious. Her response to infidelity was rather ordinary: she felt jealous, anxious, angry, rejecting and in need of someone for herself.

It was hard for Natalie's lovers to feel secure, though her friendship and caring were never in doubt. Renée refused to meet her, and sent her a strange hair ornament of a golden dragon, spewing a spray of opals. Then in winter 1901 Renée received a telegram from Nice. Violet Shiletto, gravely ill, was asking for her. She left immediately. Natalie went to tea with Opale.

7

More Renée Vivien

'Sweet Mistress of my Songs, let us go to Mytilene.'

While Renée was in Nice at Violet Shiletto's bedside, Natalie went to Venice with Opale. Opale was obsessed with Bosie. She kept a photograph of him by her bed, and a piece of his hair in a heart-shaped locket, and talked endlessly of his dire need for money and how her parents would not countenance their marriage. Natalie, with her revisionist ideas of family, offered to marry him if that might help Opale.

Renée returned to Paris devastated by the death of Violet and Natalie's betrayal. She refused to see her and poured out poems about the loss of love, dead roses and the ashes of desire.

Albert Barney had a second heart attack in the summer of 1902. Natalie went to Washington to be with her mother. 'I took up my old social round of visits, balls, flirtations, horse rides, until the sudden arrival of Alfred Douglas.' Bosie, though wearing a ring Opale had given him, was intent on finding a rich American wife, and thought Natalie would do. They went for long carriage drives, and became engaged, but her father barred him from the house, and Bosie was socially ostracised for his 'doings in London' and friendship with 'objectionable persons'. He wrote to Opale of his loathing of America and his desire to marry her for love, not twenty thousand a year.

Natalie sent telegrams and letters to Renée asking her to come to Washington. Renée declined, said she could not afford it, told Natalie to console herself with Opale and Eva Palmer, and accused her of wielding power: 'the anguish, humiliation and wounds you inflicted . . . Away from you I don't suffer the pain, anxiety and jealousy I endure when I watch you handing out smiles and provocative looks to every woman and man.'

In Paris, Renée moved into a new apartment at 23 Avenue du Bois, 'my flimsy shelter, my place of refuge and calm, a place on earth that belongs to me, where I will be mistress, ruler and entirely free'. She decorated it to lugubrious effect. Colette[1] said it smelled like a rich man's funeral. Oppressed by the dripping candles, heavy curtains, incense, and flowers, she once tried to open one of the leaded windows. It was nailed shut. Romaine Brooks described a

dark heavily-curtained room, grim life-sized Oriental figures sitting propped on chairs, phosphorescent Buddhas in folds of black draperies . . . the air heavy with incense. We lunch seated on the floor with scant food served on ancient Damascus ware, cracked and stained. During the meal Renée Vivien leaves us to bring in from the garden her pet frogs and a serpent which she twists round her wrist.

---

1 Colette (1873–1954), French novelist. The first woman president of the Académie Goncourt. Natalie, a close friend, was Miss Flossie in her novel *Claudine s'en va*.

Renée wrote to Natalie that though she loved her unchangingly, despite sadness, disillusion, and disappointment, she did not want to be tormented any more. 'You are such a complex creature, neither entirely true or false. I try to know what is true behind the lies, what is false behind the truth.'

Then Liane, in a letter to Natalie, seemed pleased to impart unwelcome news: 'Renée is with La Brioche (you know, the Baronne Hélène van Zuylen de Nyevelt).[2] La Brioche has just published a book of poetry, *Effeuillements* [Falling Leaves]'[3] The Baronne, a member of the Rothschild family, was fourteen years older than Renée, large, fabulously rich, and known as La Brioche for the way she wore her hair.

Natalie, when back in Paris, went straight to the Avenue du Bois. The concierge told her Mademoiselle was out. She waited in the courtyard. 'My heart beat wildly as I caught sight of Renée at last in her car.' She ran to meet her, but Renée instructed the chauffeur not to stop. Violet's sister, Mary Shiletto, who had the apartment above Renée's, would offer no explanation as to why Renée had driven away.

Natalie stayed for hours with Mary, watching the courtyard from her window. In the evening Renée returned with her new friend. 'The way in which she put her arms around Renée made the intimacy between them clear.' Natalie then schemed to get Renée back: she stalked her, bombarded her with letters, and sent her poems about cruel hearts and unfaithful glances. She compared the

---

2 Hélène van Zuylen (1868–1947). She was separated from her husband, played polo, raced cars, and had two children.

3 *Une éffeuilleuse* is a striptease artist.

challenge to a horse race. She would, she confessed, 'gallop wildly' in the Bois to avoid being overtaken.

Renée ignored it all. Natalie elicited help from an opera singer friend, Emma Calvé, who dressed as a busker and under Renée's window sang, 'I have lost Euridice, there is no pain like mine' from Gluck's *Orfeo ed Euridice*.[4] A crowd gathered and tossed coins. When Renée came out on her balcony to see what was going on, Natalie threw poems and flowers to her. Renée's housekeeper sent a note asking Natalie to stop these gestures, which were as useless as they were distressing.

In October 1902, Albert Barney, ill with pleurisy, asked Natalie to go with him to Monte Carlo for a cure. She was 'too tormented' over Renée to oblige, so he went alone with a nurse. Natalie's preoccupation was to see Renée. When she heard that Renée was going with Eva Palmer to the opera – *Manfred* by Schumann[5] – she contrived to take Eva's ticket. She and Renée listened, 'rapturously entwined'. Renée agreed to another meeting but did not show up. 'One can't play one's life over again,' she wrote.

On 5 December Natalie was summoned to Monte Carlo. Her father's nurse met her at the station and told her of his death. The previous night he had spoken of wanting to divorce Alice and to cut her out of his will, and had dreamed of a room filled with flowers for Natalie's wedding to Freddy Manners-Sutton. Natalie saw him dead but felt no grief. 'This peace at last attained seemed

---

4 First performed in Vienna in 1762.

5 Schumann gave it the title 'Manfred: a dramatic poem in three parts by Lord Byron with music by Robert Schumann'. It premièred in Weimar in 1852.

to warn me: Do not come too near.' She went alone to his cremation at Père Lachaise,[6] then sailed to New York with his ashes for
funeral ceremonies and estate formalities.

She returned to Paris very rich, for her share of his estate was
more than 1 million dollars. She acquired a house in Neuilly-sur-
Seine and disturbed the neighbours by staging her own plays and
tableaux vivants in the garden. In one tableau Mata Hari[7] emerged
from the bushes naked, except for a tinsel crown. In *Équivoque,*
about Sappho – choreographed by Isadora Duncan's[8] brother
Raymond – Eva Palmer, Colette, and Sacha Guitry[9] danced in thin
gauze round an incense-burning brazier. Penelope Sikelianos,
Raymond Duncan's wife, played the harp.

Though rich, Natalie was not as fabulously rich as La Brioche,
who sent messengers to the Avenue du Bois laden with presents
for Renée – a collection of ancient Persian coins, a glass cabinet
of exotic butterflies, a miniature garden of bushes with leaves of
crystal and fruit of precious stones.

Natalie could not accept she had been ousted. She followed
Renée to the Bayreuth music festival and again, by taking Eva
Palmer's ticket, contrived to sit next to her through fifteen hours
of Wagner's Ring Cycle. 'First our eyes met, then our hands in the
shadows.' She implored Renée to have her back and wrote her a

6 Père Lachaise opened as a cemetery in 1804. The crematorium was built in 1889.

7 Mata Hari (1876–1917) was five foot ten, danced in Paris, joined the German secret
   service in 1907, and was executed as a spy by the French.

8 Isadora Duncan (1877–1927). A pioneer of modern dance, she was inspired by ancient
   Greek drama, danced barefoot and had schools in Paris, Berlin, Moscow and London.
   She died when her scarf caught in the wheel of her car when she was motoring on the
   Promenade des Anglais in Nice.

9 Sacha Guitry (1885–1957), French actor, dramatist and filmmaker. His plays included
   Notto (1905) and *Mozart* (1925).

long prose poem, 'Je me souviens': 'Let us forget the days of anger and all that separates your hand from my loving hand . . . Close your eyes. Let me love you. Go mad with me, for madness is the wisdom of the shadows.' She suggested they go together to the island of Lesbos and in Grecian sunshine write poetry and emulate the Sapphic dream of love.

Her tenacity worked, Renée capitulated in the summer of 1904. They met in Vienna in August, took the Orient Express to Constantinople, then an Egyptian steamer, the *Khedire*, to Lesbos. Natalie described herself as elated, as travelling to discover not a place but a person. Renée, too, seemed fervent and on the day they arrived at Lesbos stood at the ship's prow at dawn to see the island rise from the sea.

Disaffection was swift. It was not the classical Greece of their expectations. As they docked, a stevedore called to them through a megaphone: 'Come here little chickens. Come here little chickens.' There were no myrtle groves, silver fountains, or hyacinth gardens stretching to the ocean, no women with Sappho's profile, only rough-looking fishermen and shepherds.

They had each other and no one else, there was occasional mail, but no visitors. They rented two villas joined by an orchard. In the larger of these Renée worked on her translation into French of Sappho's poems, and her own verses about Natalie's sighs, kisses, whispers, and her scent of rose and peach. An old woman cooked their food. Renée gave hers to the dog and subsisted on wine and a few figs.

Natalie viewed the island as an Aegean bed, in the sun, on great banks of seaweed. She hinted that, for the first time in their affair, Renée reached orgasm. She viewed this as a triumph, 'smothered a cry of victory' and said she had not imagined their souls and bodies could unite so deeply. They talked of plans for a lesbian community on the island, where young women 'vibrant with poetry, youth and love would come from all parts of the world'. (Pierre Louÿs' pastoral fiction of lesbian life was enhanced two years after *Songs of Bilitis* by the discovery in Egypt of a hundred fragments of Sappho's poems written on papyrus that had been used to mummify crocodiles.)

Natalie read to Renée poems about Sappho from her first book *Cinq petits dialogues grecs*. She had dedicated it to Louÿs 'from a young woman of the future society'. Sappho was more faithful in inconstancy than were others in their fidelity, Natalie told Renée. Only women were chimerical and complex enough to attract her, hold her, and offer her all ecstasy and all torment. 'Sappho is you,' Renée said.

After a month the idyll broke. Waiting for Renée at the post office in Mytilene was a letter from La Brioche demanding a meeting in Constantinople. In reply, Renée sent a telegram saying she was on her way. She voiced fear to Natalie of the tactics the Baroness might otherwise use to get her back: alert the consulates of every country, hire detectives, abduct her. 'Her power like her fortune has no limit,' she said.

Renée chose to return to the baroness's domination, but in Paris her torment over Natalie did not end. She wanted to be with her, but did not feel safe with her. She wrote letters asking for forgiveness and sent morbid poems of love: 'I have searched for your look in strangers' eyes, I have searched for your kiss on fleeting lips. I have spoiled my heart and ruined my soul.'

Natalie responded to rejection with meanness. She told Renée of an affair La Brioche was having – with a neighbour who had bought a horse from her. Renée packed her jade Buddha, withdrew her money from the bank and took a train to Marseilles, intending to leave France. La Brioche sent Natalie a one-word card, 'Judas'.

At Marseilles, La Brioche's secretary was there at the quayside to escort Renée back to Paris. The relationship with La Brioche resumed. Natalie, jealous, wrote to Eva Palmer of how her morning walks were 'harassed by the sight of their coupé[10] and steppers,[11] which makes me take to running with all agility'. But for Renée trust had gone. In 1907 La Brioche left her for another woman. Renée took other lovers, and until her death in 1909 travelled rootlessly. She went to Jerusalem, Egypt, Constantinople, Hawaii, Japan. Ill with anorexia, alcohol and drug addiction, she travelled so as never to arrive, and wrote to Natalie that she did not know how to continue her 'miserable existence'.

---

10 A short, four-wheeled carriage with an inside seat for two, and an outside seat for the driver.

11 Horses with good paces and showy action.

4

Constance had more front than Selfridges at Christmas-time. In my eighth-floor flat at King Edward Mansions the rubbish lift was hauled up at 7.45 a.m. daily, with ropes and pulleys, by Gilbert, the porter, from the courtyard below. On the day Constance[1] clambered out of it and through my kitchen window in fox fur and silver boots, I sought an injunction against her. Enough is enough. But why had Gilbert allowed it? He was so terse and dismissive. What tall story had she told him, what charm did she exert?

---

1 Constance killed herself in a Sydney hotel room in April 1983. She took amphetamine to give herself courage, then went out on barbiturates.

8

Renée Vivien's Death

'Be one of life's equals.'

Natalie was everything to her lovers for a while. But she would not offer fidelity: 'To love what one has is to be resigned to never getting what one wants,' was one of her aphorisms.

Olive eloped with Bosie in March 1902 and their son, Raymond, was born eight months later. Natalie, as his godmother, gave a christening gift of opals for him to use as marbles. The marriage, she said, was more for worse than better. Bosie, dependent on Olive's allowance, and on bad terms with her father, said he became more manly after he married and the more manly he was, the less Olive loved him. 'How could I know or guess that the very thing she loved in me was that which I was always trying to suppress and keep under: I mean the feminine part of me?'

She left him twice and the second time took all the furniture Bosie became as litigious as his father, the Marquess of Queensberry who had destroyed Oscar Wilde. Among those he sued for libel was Freddy Manners-Sutton. Litigation bankrupted him and libelling Winston Churchill earned him a prison sentence in Worm-wood Scrubs.

Raymond became the victim of their marriage. As a boy he was wrangled over by Bosie and by Olive's father, who kidnapped him and took him to Scotland. Olive showed little interest in her son. In his teens he had a psychotic breakdown and as a man he spent his life, such as it was, in institutions until he killed himself.

Eva Palmer, Natalie's first lover, went to Greece with Raymond Duncan and his wife Penelope Sikelianos in 1905. She began a relationship with Penelope's brother, the poet, Angelos Sikelianos, and told Natalie she was going to marry him, live in Greece, and stage Greek drama, dance and music.[2] Natalie, who was used to Eva 'bending to her least desire', tried to dissuade her. Eva assured her she loved her more than anyone: 'Oh hands that I have loved, eyes that I have followed, hair that I have sobbed to touch,' but she was tired of her 'intrigues and passions'. 'I have walked after you for years, like a high-heeled woman whose feet hurt, but who is too proud to say so.'

Of Renée, Natalie said she could live neither with her nor without her. 'I tried in vain to save her. She could not be saved. Her life was a long suicide. Everything turned to dust and ashes in her hands.' But in their time together Renée wrote fourteen volumes of poems that did not turn to dust. Her poetry disarmed the indignation of moralists. Into it went her conflict with Natalie, her mourning of Violet Shiletto's death, her romantic despair.

To Colette, Renée alluded to sexual tyranny and control from

2 His manuscripts and her costume designs are now at the Angelos and Eva Sikelianos Museum in Delphi, where they staged their plays.

her over-rich keeper, La Baronne van Zuylen. 'With her I dare not pretend or lie, because at that moment she lays her ear over my heart.' That moment was, it seemed, the point of orgasm. 'There are fewer ways of making love than they say,' Renée told Colette 'and more than one believes.' La Baronne, she implied, knew them all.

In *The Pure and the Impure*[3] Colette wrote of how, in the middle of a dinner Renée was giving – little strips of raw fish rolled on glass wands, tiny bits of foie gras on plates of jade, exotic cocktails and expensive champagne – she left her guests, whispering, 'I am requisitioned. She is terrible at present.'

Colette observed the symptoms of Renée's anorexia: how she would not be seen drinking, eating – or writing poetry. She caught her secretly gulping wine then rinsing her mouth in rose water. She saw her faint with inanition between sentences, her chin on her thin chest, her eyes closed, her hands open and lifeless on the tablecloth. She saw her scribbling on a writing pad then spring up guiltily and say, 'It's nothing, I've finished now.'

Once they went together to Pascaud's to hire costumes for a fancy-dress ball at the Théâtre des Arts. Renée was to be Lady Jane Grey ready for execution. After her fitting, she put on Colette's black coat by mistake. Colette, who was plump, commented that the coat almost fitted. Renée responded with panic. She must, she said, lose ten pounds in the ten days before the ball. Though tall she would not allow herself to weigh more than seven stone. She booked in at a clinic in St Germain. In the mornings she drank

---

3 First published in Paris in 1932 with the title *Ces plaisirs* . . . and structured as a dialectic into the nature and laws of erotic life.

a glass of tea, then walked ten miles in the forest. In the evenings she had more tea with alcohol added. She was at the ball, sylph-like, with shadows under her eyes. After it she fainted backstage.

Natalie moved on to new affairs – with Colette, with Henriette Roggers, an actress whom she pursued to St Petersburg – but for years she hoped for reconciliation with Renée, a new beginning, freed from past mistakes.

In 1909 she was evicted from her home in Neuilly, after her land-lord read an article in *Comoedia* about nude women cavorting in her shady garden in the spirit of Bilitis and Sappho. Her new house, at 20 rue Jacob, was to be her home until she died. Heavy double doors opened to a cobbled courtyard at the end of which was a two-storeyed eighteenth-century house set in a walled overgrown garden, with a tall chestnut tree. In a corner of the garden was a small Doric temple with TEMPLE À L'AMITIÉ inscribed over its entrance. In this temple to friendship, in a leafy garden in the heart of Paris, Natalie hoped to recreate with Renée the Sapphic dream.

In November, some months after she had moved, she heard that Renée was ill. She went at once to her apartment. A butler whom she had not seen before opened the door and said 'Mademoiselle has just died'. Natalie asked him to put beside Renée the violets she had brought, then, in the Avenue du Bois, she fainted on a bench.

Renée was thirty-one when she died and weighed under six stone. At death's brink she converted to Catholicism with the romantic anticipation of meeting Violet Shiletto once more. Natalie, with wry competitiveness, remarked that Jesus Christ had seduced more women than Don Juan. She translated into English the poem Renée wrote for her own tomb:

Here is the gate through which I leave
Oh my roses and my thorns
What matter now days gone by?
I sleep and dream of things divine
Herein lies my ravished soul
It is peaceful sleeping now
Having for the love of Death
Forgiven the bitter crime of Life

5

Nicki chose a crab omelette, lamb with butter beans, a lime pie. She drank wine and a Gaelic coffee then left the table. She was thinner than anyone should want to be. You and I talked of our mothers and of palliative care. When she came back her eyes were bloodshot. Asked by you how fat she thought her arms were – 'That fat?' you suggested, holding your hands apart, she replied 'Fatter.' 'That fat?' You widened the space to the girth of an elephant's thigh. 'Fatter.'

She sipped some water. We asked for the bill.

6

You say we should not blame our mothers for our shortcomings, now that we are both women of a certain age . . . Then whose fault is it that you get so stoned, fritter your money and carry on with that antiquarian bookbinder from Lausanne?

9

Rue Jacob

'My queerness is not a vice, is not deliberate, and harms no one.'

In December 1902, when Natalie arrived in New York with her father's ashes, her mother was at the quayside wearing a black crépe hat with feathers. They laughed as they embraced. 'How wildly our hearts beat alike,' Natalie said.

Alice, now forty-five and liberated from her husband's disapproval of all she did, was full of plans to make Washington the cultural capital of the western world. She set about financing and designing Studio House in Massachusetts Avenue as a showcase for contemporary American art. It was to have galleries, musicians' halls and a huge studio. Her pastels and portraits were to hang beside those of Joshua Reynolds[1] and James Whistler. She shared Natalie's liking for categorical thought. VICI CALAMITAEM LABORE – work conquers disasters – was fired in tiles in the hallway. It should have read CALAMITATEM, but her design had not allowed for grout. Stencilled in gold on the studio walls was: THE HIGHEST

---

1 Joshua Reynolds (1723–92), English portrait painter and president of the Royal Academy when it was established in 1768.

PROBLEM OF ART IS TO PRODUCE BY APPEARANCE THE ILLUSION OF
HIGHER REALITY.

Neighbours complained when a sculpture by Laura Barney of
Natalie reclining naked was exhibited on the front lawn. The police
ordered it to be covered up, so Alice put it in a tent, but it got
stolen in the night and reappeared in Washington Square next to
General Sheridan on his horse.[2] The story was picked up by the
national papers.

Alice had formidable enthusiasm and energy. She produced and
directed *The Dream of Queen Elizabeth* and *Romeo and Juliet* with
Eva Palmer as Romeo; she wrote and starred in *The Man in the
Moon* and *The Bridal Veil;* she staged tableaux in which, scantily
clad, she danced like a dervish, and operettas for which she had
written the libretti. She set up a centre for decorative arts, Neigh-
borhood House, where she taught tie-dyeing. When elected Vice-
President of the Society of Washington Artists, she was seldom
out of the society columns. There were pictures of her at her first
nights in black tulle patterned with peacock eyes, or peering through
a diamond-studded lorgnette, with ostrich plumes in her hair.

Natalie's love affairs bewildered her, but with a flourish she
espoused the cause of women's suffrage and feminism. In 1913 she
loaned one of her houses, at 1626 Rhode Island Avenue, to the
National American Women's Suffrage Association as its Washington
headquarters. To show her allegiance she wrote didactic plays. *The
Woman* starred Izetta Jewell as 'Woman', bound to a bush by 'Sin',
'Ignorance' and 'Man' (played by Christian Hemmick). 'Freedom'

2 General Sheridan said his black horse, Rienzi, ridden by him in the Civil War, was 'an
animal of great intelligence and immense strength and endurance'.

then conjured scenes showing the achievements of Sappho, Esther, Queen Zenobia, Elizabeth of Hungary, St Hilda, Joan of Arc, Angelica Kauffman, Charlotte Corday, Jane Austen, and Kurerat Elayn, a Persian women's rights martyr.

Christian Hemmick was given the male lead in most of her productions. He bleached his hair, used perfume and fancied young male dancers. Alice called him her 'pink pet'. In 1909 when she was fifty-two and he was twenty-two she left with him for Paris, to introduce him to her daughters before marrying him. Natalie asked, tersely, why her mother wanted to tie herself to another man, particularly a pederast. Laura thought him a gigolo, who was after her mother's money.

Laura and Alice had a double wedding. Laura's husband, Hippolyte Dreyfus, was a professor of oriental studies and leader of the Bahai movement in Paris.[3] Hemmick, to show he was marrying Alice for love, signed a deposition renouncing his right to any part of her fortune. They went to the Dolomites for their honeymoon, but he complained about her habit of getting up at six in the morning and going to bed at nine-thirty every evening, leaving him alone with Balzac's letters to Madame Hanska.[4]

The marriage was not a success. Alice worked with alarming zeal while her husband lounged around. Her wealth and productiveness emphasised his inadequacy. As an actor he received poor reviews. Alice made out large cheques to him, and encouraged and financed his passing enthusiasms for unlikely business ventures.

---

3 Hippolyte Dreyfus translated from Arabic to French the message of the prophet Bah-Ullah. Bahaists keep their own creed – Buddhist, Christian, etc., but emphasise the universality of faith over doctrine.

4 Honoré de Balzac (1790–1850) was in love with Eveline Hanska, a rich Polish aristocrat, for the last fifteen years of his life. He married her in March 1850 but died three months later.

One of these was a scheme to manufacture and market scented household cleaning pastes. He took salt and abrasives from the scullery, mixed them with Alice's perfumes, and designed labels for their jars. She set him up in an office, but instead of working he wrote letters on scented notepaper to pretty young men.

By 1918 Alice wanted a divorce. Hemmick protested that he was a Catholic and that marriage was a divine contract. Natalie castigated her mother for her lavishness toward this 'worthless boy pederast husband and the thousands of dollars wasted on him'. When Alice learned of an affair he was having in Pittsburgh with the dancer Paul Swan, she told him the marriage was over and that she would be writing no more cheques.

She reverted to being Mrs Barney. When she sent out 'At Home' cards from her house at Rhode Island Avenue, the *Washington Times* for 21 November 1919 ran a front-page article: 'Society Leader Discards Husband's Name'. Hemmick agreed to divorce on the grounds of desertion if she gave him $10,000, which she did in 1920, together with a lawyer's letter stating she owed him nothing more. She then sailed for Paris.

Natalie equalled her mother's cultural ambitions. Her aspiration was to make her TEMPLE À L'AMITIÉ the Sapphic centre of the Western world. She felt no need to court society's approval: 'What do I care if they vilify me or judge me according to their prejudices.' If her guests were women who dressed as wood nymphs, shepherdesses or court pages, if they danced naked or in gauze, if they kissed and more, it was fine by her.

From October 1909, each Friday when Natalie was in Paris, she held an afternoon salon at rue Jacob from four to eight. It was at heart a lesbian arts club, where writers, painters, and poets felt at ease. Freud, Krafft-Ebing and Havelock Ellis[5] had pathologised homosexuality, writers like Compton Mackenzie[6] mocked it, lawmakers criminalised it and the Bloomsbury Group euphemised it. Radclyffe Hall apologised glumly about being a 'congenital invert', Gertrude Stein described herself as a husband with Alice B. Toklas as her wife, Vita Sackville-West praised marriage but pursued same-sex affairs . . .[7] Natalie revised attitudes. She extolled the kiss of the fictional Bilitis. 'I am a lesbian,' she said. 'One need not hide it, nor boast of it, though being other than normal is a perilous advantage.' With Sappho as her guide she lived the advantages and made light of the perils. 'They say it is necessary to conform. I have never conformed, nevertheless I exist.'

At Natalie's salons, women could embrace, hold hands, be open about desire. Men were admitted, but were not allowed to dominate the afternoons. After 1927 the Friday gatherings focused on the work of women. Natalie styled these meetings the *Académie des Femmes* as a snook at the all-male *Académie Française*.[8] Sylvia Beach, who ran the bookshop Shakespeare and Company at 12 rue de l'Odéon, said, 'At Miss Barney's one met lesbians; Paris ones and those only passing through town, ladies with high collars and monocles, though Miss Barney herself was so feminine.'

Natalie's salon style came from her resolve to live life as a work

---

5 Sigmund Freud, *Three Essays on the Theory of Sexuality,* 1905. Richard von Krafft-Ebing, *Psychopathia Sexualis, 1886* (237 case histories). Havelock Ellis, *Sexual Inversion,* 1897.

6 Compton Mackenzie (1883–1972), Scottish novelist. In 1928 he wrote *Extraordinary Women,* a satire of lesbians on Capri.

7 Vita Sackville-West (1892–1962) locked away in a Gladstone bag her account of her love for Violet Trefusis. It was annotated after Violet's death, in 1973, by Vita's son, Nigel Nicolson, and published as *Portrait of a Marriage.*

8 Natalie's friend, the novelist Marguerite Yourcenar (1903–87), was the first woman to be admitted to the Académie Française in 1980.

of art. At 20 rue Jacob art and life entwined. Having money freed her from caring about money. Nor did she burden herself with possessions: 'I dread possessions because they possess you,' she said. Or 'I can live without fear of robbers. You can't rob an atmosphere.'

Instead she collected people. They gathered in her ground-floor salon, its walls covered in red damask that faded down the years, its domed ceiling painted with nymphs. The furniture was cast-offs from her mother: Spanish chairs, an Empire couch, a marble table, red curtains. Paintings were for association not value: portraits of her friends by her mother, her portrait as the Happy Prince by Carolus-Duran. In an alcove was a bust of Watteau[9] given to her by Robert de Montesquiou.[10] Liane de Pougy's influence showed in the all-blue bedroom. On the floor was the polar-bear rug, at the windows were lawn curtains embroidered with MAY OUR DRAWN CURTAINS SHIELD US FROM THE WORLD.

In the dining room, which led to the garden, was a large oval centre table, set with a tea urn, glass pitchers of fruit juice, triangular sandwiches, little cakes from Rumpelmayer's.[11] On a marble buffet were fruits, port and whisky. Before Berthe Cleyrergue arrived in June 1927 and became Natalie's 'librarian, manager, receptionist, nurse, handyman and [above all] cook', domestic helpers came and

---

9 Jean-Antoine Watteau (1684–1721), French rococo painter.

10 Comte Robert de Montesquiou (1855–1921). Descended from an ancient French family, he introduced Natalie to Parisian society. He wrote ornate symbolic poetry. His homosexual lifestyle inspired Proust's Baron de Charlus in À la Recherche du Temps Perdu and he was the model for Des Esseintes in J.K. Huysman's A Rebours. In his will he left Natalie a Persian tapestry, which she hung on the wall in her dining room.

11 A belle-époque salon-de-thé on the rue de Rivoli with gilded mouldings, marble tables and frescoed walls. It was opened by an Austrian, Antoine Rumpelmayer, in 1903. Gertrude Stein liked his honey cake.

went. Natalie said she preferred them a little blind and deaf. Her Chinese butler painted curlicues on his bald pate.

'I didn't create a salon,' said Natalie. 'A salon was created around me.' Paul Valéry[12] called these gatherings 'the hazardous Fridays', they were so unpredictable. Inspired by Natalie's candour, they were a showcase for artistic innovation that continued for sixty years. No creative effort that interested her, however bizarre, was spurned. 'The universe came here,' Edmond Jaloux[13] wrote, 'from San Francisco to Japan, from Lima to Moscow, from London to Rome.'

Often Natalie arrived late; usually she wore white. She looked for and encouraged talent, and gave patronage. American writers found French translators, poets found publishers. Many of her guests had been, or would be her lovers: Liane de Pougy, Elisabeth de Gramont, Elizabeth Eyre de Lanux,[14] who lived next door and was impressed by the visitors to Natalie's temple, Lucie Delarue-Mardrus, who in 1930 wrote *The Angel and the Pervert* in which she portrayed Natalie as a fantasist who lived for seduction in wealth and idleness.

Down the years the list of visitors accrued, a compendium of artists. To Natalie's 'dazzling Fridays' they brought their creations: their poems, stories, dances, quartets, and songs. Gertrude Stein, Colette, and Edith Sitwell[15] read work in progress. Pierre Louÿs

---

12 Paul Valéry (1871–1945), French poet, critic and essayist. With André Gide and Pierre Louÿs he created the literary reviews *La Conque* and *Le Centaure*. Natalie first met him in Lily de Gramont's bomb shelter, in 1917, when he was reciting his poem *La Jeune Parque*. It had 512 verses and even he described it as obscure.

13 Edmond Jaloux (1878–1949), French novelist and literary critic and biographer of Rainer Maria Rilke.

14 Elizabeth Eyre de Lanux (1894–1996), American artist, fresco painter, interior designer and writer.

15 Edith Sitwell (1887–1964), English poet, sister to Osbert and Sacheverell. She was painted by John Singer Sargent. From 1916 to 1921 she edited *Wheels,* an annual anthology of modern verse.

brought André Gide[16] and Paul Valéry. Natalie's teacher, Charles Brun, brought the critic Salomon Reinach. And so it snowballed. Romaine Brooks, Janet Flanner,[17] Djuna Barnes, Dolly Wilde, Nancy Cunard,[18] Peggy Guggenheim,[19] Radclyffe Hall, Ezra Pound,[20] T.S.Eliot,[21] Gabriele D'Annunzio,[22] Rabindranath Tagore,[23] Jean Cocteau, Rainer Maria Rilke,[24] all called at Natalie's salon for the cutting edge of art, and strawberry tarts.

As a frontispiece to *Pensées d'une Amazone* published in 1921, Natalie used a rough doodle of her temple, with À L'AMITIÉ scrawled across its doors, and below it her dining room. Crammed into every space and spilling out into the garden she wrote in higgledy-piggledy script the names of those who had been to her Fridays. Each name spoke of an individual and a contribution to modernism. Making threads of connection, drawing these disparate names together, weaving in and out among them, was Natalie, the Amazon.

16 André Gide (1869–1951), French novelist, playwright and critic, winner of the Nobel Prize for Literature in 1947.

17 Janet Flanner (1892–1978), American columnist who wrote as 'Genêt'. In October 1925 she published her first 'Letter from Paris' in the *New Yorker.* Solita Solano, her partner, was drama editor of the *New York Tribune.* They met in 1918.

18 Nancy Cunard (1896–1965), rich patron, socialite and alcoholic. She founded the Hours Press in 1927 and published Ezra Pound, Laura Riding, and Samuel Beckett. She began a relationship with Henry Crowder, a black American jazz musician in 1928.

19 Peggy Guggenheim (1898–1979), American heiress and patron of modern art. She housed collections of art in museums in Venice and New York. She married Max Ernst to give him American citizenship. Her father, Ben Guggenheim, went down on the Titanic in 1912.

20 Ezra Pound (1885–1972), American imagist poet who settled in Britain. He was the London editor of the *Little Review* in 1917. A fascist, he was arrested for treason in the Second World War.

21 T.S. Eliot (1888–1965), born in the US he took British citizenship in 1927. He won the Nobel Prize for Literature in 1948.

22 Gabriele D'Annunzio (1863–1938), Italian dramatist, military hero, and political leader.

23 Rabindranath Tagore (1861–1941), Indian poet, awarded the Nobel Prize for Literature in 1913, the first Asian to receive this.

24 Rainer Maria Rilke (1875–1926), German lyric poet.

7

In a basement in Camden Town blond Madame Givenchy[1] sang There's
Something About a Soldier *and strutted the stage. His long crimson
frock was matched by long crimson nails. His punchline, much repeated,
was 'I'm not a vindictive old queen.'*

'Oh yes you are,' his audience replied.

*His face had sharpness and no repose. I shared a table with Olave
and Elise. They shared a love of artefact, a passion for make-up and
clothes, a strategic evasion of heart or time. My eyes worked to correct
their deceptions. 'I'm not a vindictive old queen,' chanted Madame
Givenchy. Oh yes you are. You have become what you are not.*

---

1 Madame Givenchy, aka Mervyn Carpenter, died of AIDS on 8 September 1986 in the
Patrick Manson Unit at the Middlesex Hospital.

10

Rémy de Gourmont

'You are a true friend and I love you.'

Rémy de Gourmont[1] took Natalie from the margins of French culture and made her iconic. He was the author of a hundred volumes of fiction, verse and essays, and founder of and leading contributor to the literary journal, *Le Mercure de France*. In 1910, a neighbour, the publisher Edouard Champion, showed him Natalie's poems about the death of Renée Vivien. De Gourmont thought highly of them and published them. Flattered, Natalie sent him a book of her epigrams *Éparpillements* [Scatterings]. He read and reread them, and wrote to her that she was a noble and sensitive soul with whom he felt in sympathy even when she was enigmatic: 'One should remain an enigma, even to oneself.'

They met, and with the desperation of infirmity and a romantic heart, he fell in love with her. He was in his fifties and a hermit. As a young man he had contracted a form of lupus, which ravaged

---

1 Rémy de Gourmont (1858–1915), principal critic of the Symbolist movement, born at Château de la Motte, Bazoches-en-Houlmes in Normandy.

his appearance and weakened his muscles. Natalie described his clear blue eyes as 'like two children living in a ruin'. He lived ten minutes walk from her at 71 rue des Saints-Pères in a garret up six flights of winding stairs. She visited him there on Sunday afternoons. Until she breezed like springtime into his life, his horizons were the offices of the *Mercure de France*, the second-hand booksellers on the Quai Voltaire by the Seine, and the Café de Flore.

Natalie coaxed him out of his book-lined cell. 'Too weak in body for pleasure, too clear-sighted to be ambitious, it did him good to sail away on the arms of an Amazon.' For their third meeting she sent her chauffeur to collect him in the evening. 'He climbed into my Renault without too much trouble despite its wide running boards.' She took him to the Bois, there was a full moon and the scent of acacias, he told her that were he to see diamonds sparkling on the ground he would not pick them up for he had no one to give them to.

For him, she was a consuming passion, for her, she gave him some of her time. He spoke of cherished moments with her, 'a hundred little happinesses'. He wrote of an evening spent sitting in her garden: he had drunk a glass of lemon and water, the tree they sat under made lacework patterns against the sky, he admired her face in shadow in the darkness, the lights of Paris glowed, she said trifling things that made him laugh, a startled cat leaped into the tree, he heard its claws on the bark, then silence.

She gave a party for him at her house, a masked ball so his disfigurement was concealed. She disguised him as an Arab with one of her green silk stockings wrapped around his head. She went as a Japanese glow-worm chaser adorned with sprays of little lights. 'Men,' he wrote of the evening, 'show more of their true selves when wearing a disguise. It is perhaps in their daily lives that they wear the thickest mask.'

He expressed his love for Natalie in print. Every fortnight from January 1912 until October 1913 he published a letter to her in *Le Mercure de France*. He called these *Lettres à l'Amazone* and in them he extolled her, not least for all the good feelings he found in himself through her. The Amazon was his sobriquet for her, because often she visited wearing jodhpurs and boots after riding in the Bois.

On their Sundays when she rang the bell – always twice – he pulled her through the door to his apartment as though rescuing her from danger. By this door was a tapestry of a viper, his opinion of the outside world. He said whenever he saw her he felt a quickening of his heart. It was proof to him that he still had a heart. He watched her closely as she scrutinised the draft of his fortnightly letters. She was his reader. 'You are the only person,' he told her, 'to whom I have ever submitted if not my feelings at least my intelligence. If I dared, I would have you read everything I write.'

When she left, he stood on the landing in the dim gaslight and watched her go down the long spiral staircase. When she reached the courtyard she always looked up. He was always still there. She never saw his door close.

He admitted that sex was on his mind, but he liked concealed desire, 'like ultraviolet rays unperceived by eyes'. Were he able to have a lover, he said, were it possible, he would choose her, Amazon though she was and unattracted to him. Once, she reached across the table in his study and put her hand over his hands, which were dry like parchment but had a warmth that surprised her.

Through these published letters Natalie became the Amazon of Rémy de Gourmont. Such a profile confused many, including her mother, who wanted to know what she had been doing with this old gentleman to be so talked about all over Europe. For Natalie it proved a public distraction from her affairs with Ilse Deslandes,[2] who modelled for Burne-Jones,[3] or with an Armenian dancer, Armen Ohanian,[4] whom she pursued to St Petersburg.

Despite such 'absorbing passions' as she called them, she did not fail her friendship with de Gourmont or scorn 'his touching constancy with regard to me, if not mine toward him'. Nor did he dwell on the detail of such passions. What he loved was her free spirit, her fervour for conquest and love, her energy and air of the outdoors, her unavailability. He was quintessentially French but in his letters to her, he aspired to go beyond both language and gender. He wanted obscure expression, paradox, contradiction, in an endeavour to reach meaning. 'A trace of yellow goes to yellow, a trace of red goes to red.'

He occupied, he said, a shadowy place, somewhere between the horror of life and the horror of death. Looking into her eyes was his liberation, for they took him into her world. It delighted him to talk to her of love. He felt she understood him, or made an approximation to do so. He compared his days to the sea's tides; times of sands in sunlight, times when waves buried all his hopes.

---

2 The writer André Rouveyre, a friend of de Gourmont, taught Natalie and the Baronne Ilse Deslandes to dance the tango.

3 Edward Burne-Jones (1833–98), British pre-Raphaelite painter, designer and book illustrator. He called his paintings romantic dreams 'of something that never was, never will be, in light better than ever shone'.

4 Armen Ohanian's autobiography, *Dancer of Shamakha,* was published in 1918. Her father was murdered by Cossacks and her mother forced her into a brutal marriage. She escaped to Paris, worked as a courtesan, and liked smoking opium.

He did not know which frame of mind he preferred: 'Hope is a great encumbrance.'

From his Amazon, he learned that there was a will in love. Will, for him, had played a small part in his life. At the slightest resistance he had abandoned desire and retreated into silence and his own pursuits. 'If I were younger I should try to train myself according to your method.' He saw her as defended by her spirit against the cruelties of chance. 'You want to create everything about you with your own hands and only allow the flowers you choose to flourish.'

He called her Narcissus, the supreme proponent of love. 'Let us discover,' he wrote, 'the neglected truth that we love only ourselves, that we love only the idea we form of ourselves as seen by the person we desire.' Natalie, he said, wanted living eyes, not those reflected in a pool, in the eyes of the women she loved she saw herself altered and made beautiful.

De Gourmont, too, took an image of her and reflected it favourably to her, a complex image of words, intentions, and dreams. His lodgings, he said, were lit by her smile. She came into his solitude but did not break it. He liked her bold intelligence, the fact that she was not dashed by anything. He thought what he called the male and female aspects of her nature to be so closely mingled that he never knew how she would respond. 'My dear friend, I very often carry away from our talks the germ of one of these letters, in which I return you your opinions mingled with mine, as I should like our minds always to be mingled.'

He felt they both had pagan souls, beyond Christian morality. He spoke of the 'licentious decency' of provincial towns. Religion, he said, was the plagiary of and substitute for human love. 'Each lover holds in their arms their god and the creator of their joy.' It was an echo of Natalie's scathing epigrams about God: 'The spiritually poor shall see God; the spiritually rich shall be God.' 'No wonder that His worshippers stay true to Him, they never see Him.' Human love, they both believed, was heaven. AMOR CURRIT, VOLAT ET LAETATUR. Love runs, flies and delights. In love there was no distinction between the natural and the abnormal. He praised her lack of remorse.

His letters were like conversation, touching lightly on things, passing from one association to another. In her company he ceased to be a sad man with a face disfigured by lupus. 'Eyes give, eyes take, eyes speak. We carry away nothing. We die. Let me gaze at the eyes which will survive me so that I may engrave in them the image of what I was when I dreamed this.'

He became accustomed to expressing his uncensored thoughts to her. Liberty of mind concerned him as liberty of mind and body concerned her. She caused his thoughts and inspired them. 'When I have the prospect of spending a few moments of the day near you, I feel that life is good.' He wanted his readers to be women, or men with a feminine soul like his own. He reminded her that many women followed with passionate interest the letters he wrote to her from his solitude. One woman rebuked him for expecting readers like her to collude in praising his Amazon.

He knew he was dealing with melancholy, that he was hoping and waiting for some miracle that did not exist. 'Do you remember that little phrase in one of my earliest books "And I am waiting for the person who will never come"? I am still waiting.' Natalie made his imminent death less hard. 'Devastated of flesh, in revolt against God, resisting all belief systems, he found religion in this intimacy of mind.' It suited him that she had come too late and was unavailable and unobtainable. When he was young he had loved nature. In his mind he could still hear, he said, the sound of rain on beech trees, the gentler sound of rain on lime leaves. He listened to his Amazon's dream of living wild and free in the forest, and on the wings of his imagination he went with her.

8

Do you remember when you booked a room with a 'king-size' bed in that New York hotel, high up, with a view of the park, and a bellboy took us to a gloomy twin-bedded room? And that hotel in the Wye Valley where they tried not to let us in at all. The fuss you made while I loitered. In small ways we are insulted. Would that there were more like you, more like Natalie, the Amazon, riding her horse in the Bois de Boulogne, wooing her lovers with open bouquets. You who dare not see the world as I do. Out of my way.[1]

---

1 But in an unpublished piece Natalie wrote of a room at an inn near the New Forest where she and a lover mussed the sheets of the unused second bed. Now I'm pleased to say, by way of an update, such hotel bigotry is against the law.

11

Lily de Gramont

'It is better to be a lover, than to love a lover.'

In 1910 Natalie began another of her liaisons, her serious love affairs. It was with Elisabeth de Gramont,[1] known as 'Lily', the daughter of the Duc de Gramont and Princesse Isabelle de Beauvau-Craon. Her mother died giving birth to her, her father then married Marguerite de Rothschild, and with his new wife's enormous wealth built the Château Vallières at Morte-fontaine. Lily was brought up with all the lavishness of French aristocratic life: servants, banquets, footmen, and the assumptions of her class. Proust, a good friend of hers, consulted her when writing *À la Recherche du Temps Perdu*, for detail about the placing of guests at dinner and the proper serving of food.

Lily, sophisticated and cultured, had blue eyes, a clear complexion, wore elegant dresses and plumed hats and was thought beautiful.

---

1 Also known as the Duchesse de Clermont-Tonnerre. She was descended from Henri IV (1553–1610). The gardens of her Paris house at 67 and 69 rue Raynouard stretched down to the Seine. She wrote four volumes of memoirs and dedicated her *Almanack des Bonnes Choses de France* to Natalie.

She was near-sighted and used a lorgnette. At twenty-one she married the Marquis Philibert de Clermont-Tonnerre, a reactionary, dictatorial man who tried to bend her to his views. She spoke of him as a cruel gaoler.

At heart she was as cultured and free-thinking as Natalie – who seduced her on 1 May 1910. The date became their anniversary. Lily described her love for Natalie as 'a new planet'. For a time they kept their relationship secret from the marquis, who supposed it to be innocent. That summer Natalie hired a boat, *Le Druide*, for a romantic holiday with Lily. For three days Rémy de Gourmont joined them. They sailed the coast of Normandy and each evening harboured at a little port so that he could sleep at an inn while Natalie moored alone with Lily.

With de Gourmont Natalie visited the Benedictine abbey of St-Wandrille, west of Rouen; it had been restored by Maurice Maeterlinck[2] who spent his summers there. Maeterlinck, symbolist poet and dramatist, author of the Symbolist drama *Pelléas et Mélisande* and *The Blue Bird*, talked to de Gourmont about Latin mystical writing, but seemed more interested in shooting at birds from the abbey walls while his eighteen-year-old lover, Renée Dahon, thirty-one years younger than he, replenished the cartridges of his gun.

De Gourmont went back to his 'heart of ashes' and his letters: 'My beloved friend, I see you as my final happiness and the reward for my whole life. Only your existence makes it bearable to me.' Natalie continued her boating holiday with Lily. They sailed on down the river Yonne to Mantes-la-Ville. When they parted, Natalie

---

2 Maurice Maeterlinck (1862–1949) lived with the singer Georgette Leblanc for twenty-two years then married Renée Dahon. Georgette became the lover of Margaret Anderson, editor of *The Little Review*. Debussy created his opera from *Pelléas et Mélisande* in 1902.

wrote to Lily of 'your wonderful arms about me . . . Your eyes, your voice, the maddening sweetness of you close . . . My love and your love together, safe for an hour. Sweet, when will you come again, when will you come for ever?'

Philibert de Clermont-Tonnerre divined what was going on and locked his wife in his eighteenth-century château at Glisolles. She escaped with their two daughters, Béatrix and Diane, went first to live with Natalie at the rue Jacob, then moved to a house in Passy. He divorced her in 1920. Radclyffe Hall said of her that she had left everything for Natalie: 'husband, children, home; facing scandal, opprobrium, persecution'.

Love between Natalie and Lily de Gramont evolved into a life-long friendship of respect and liking. Liane de Pougy remarked that though Lily shed bitter tears over Natalie, they both over-came jealousy. Each thought the other witty, kind, beautiful, coura-geous. Freed from the repression of her past, Lily voiced feminist and left-wing views, and earned herself the nickname the Red Duchess. She wrote volumes of memoirs in which she chronicled the social life of the Faubourg St Germain. Janet Flanner, who as Genêt wrote a column about Paris for the *New Yorker*, commended her writing for its modernity. Lily was one of the first Parisian lesbians to crop her hair short. Her friend Gertrude Stein copied her. She said to Alice B. Toklas, 'Cut it off.' Alice did not know how to go about it, or when to stop. After two days, Gertrude did not have much hair left.

Events of 1914 intruded into all their lives: the ambitions of the German Empire, the assassination of the heir to the Habsburg throne, the declaration of war on France by Germany on 4 August. Natalie believed war to be an 'extreme form of male aggression

. . . Those who *love* war lack the love of an adequate sport – the art of living.'

When Germany invaded France, Alice Barney wanted her daughters to return to Washington. Natalie had her luggage shipped from Le Havre on one of the last transatlantic liners to sail. Paris became a city of blackouts, fuel and food shortages and Zeppelin alarms, and Lily moved to her country cottage at Honfleur.[3] Lucie Mardrus had an eighteenth-century house nearby called *Pavillon de la Reine*. Both women urged Natalie to stay in France. 'You were with us in peace, you won't leave us now there is to be a war?'

De Gourmont, too, was devastated at the thought of her going. 'No more Sundays, adieu my dream. At the mention of the word journey I am filled with anguish.' So though her luggage had gone, Natalie moved to Honfleur too. 'To think about and prepare for war is boring,' she wrote to her mother. 'I'd rather live with the French even in wartime than with any other nation in time of peace.'

De Gourmont died after a stroke on 27 September 1915. He was fifty-seven. Natalie did not visit him when he was critically ill, go to his funeral, or see his grave, but neither did she betray his friendship, withdraw her permission for him to love her, or provoke his melancholy. To the end he stayed sustained by his love for her, observing its masochism, teasing the truth from his distant regard: 'Masochism is psychological before it is material, delicate before it is brutal, amorous of melancholy before it falls in love with blows and nails.'

---

3 A fishing port in Normandy, painted by Monet, with a fifteenth-century wooden church, St Catherine's.

'The great Sappho, did she not live in harmony with not one but several women?' Neighbours complained about Natalie Barney's Sapphic rituals in her Paris garden, circa 1907.

Natalie as Prince Charming, circa 1900.

'I knew little of the demi-monde. I imagined that this woman was in danger.' Natalie's lover, Liane de Pougy (1869–1950), courtesan of the Belle Epoque.

'You are the suffering that makes happiness contemptible.' Renée Vivien as the Prince with Natalie, her Muse, circa 1900.

'My door and my arms are always open to you', Colette (1873–1954), draped with a panther skin, languishing on a lion skin.

Natalie, the Amazon, circa 1907 in riding habit. Each morning she rode bareback in the Bois de Boulogne.

Natalie's mother, Alice, aged fifty-eight, full of plans to make Washington the cultural capital of the western world and with a husband thirty years her junior.

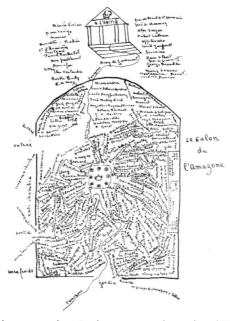

'I didn't create a salon. A salon was created round me.' Like a calligramme by Apollinaire, Natalie doodled the names of those who attended her Friday gatherings at 20 rue Jacob.

'A creature of genius with perfect legs.' Ida Rubinstein (1885–1960) as Zobeida in Diaghilev's 1910 production of Schéhérazade.

Dolly Wilde (1899–1941). 'Half androgyne, half goddess, no one's presence could be as present as Dolly's.'

'I was never a lesbian, I only loved Thelma Wood.' Djuna Barnes (1892–1982) author of *The Ladies Almanack* and *Nightwood*.

Bryher (Winifred Ellerman 1894–1983) took her name from one of the
Scilly Isles. She loved Hilda Doolittle 'so madly it is terrible'.

'I could but choose to face the future alone.'
Romaine in 1908 aged thirty-four.

Romaine kept this large painting of Ida Rubinstein (1885–1960) in her Nice studio. Romaine Brooks, *The Crossing*, circa 1911. Also called *The Passing*, *Death* and *Femme Morte* (oil on canvas, 115 x 191cm).

'Each of us lives with our dead and keeps them alive in ourselves,' Natalie wrote. De Gourmont's style of love was not hers. She liked flirting, assignation, and culmination between the sheets. By 1915 she was in pursuit of a new woman. It was not that she had tired of Lily, far from it; they remained lovers. But if there were components missing, they were of unavailability and instability. Lily was too balanced and too civilised.

At a tea party arranged by Lady Anglesey, Natalie met Romaine Brooks. Romaine had heard of Natalie's wild reputation and wanted to meet her. She was a portrait painter, American, good-looking, and very rich. She was also emotionally damaged, with a perversity that Natalie was drawn to and understood.

9

Meeting you seemed like such good luck, such passion. You laughed at my jokes, liked the way I looked. You were at my bedside when I surfaced from the anaesthetic. You said, no matter what happens I will be there for you. So when we again took my mother to lunch, to that bistro in Nether Hapcote – champagne to start, oysters for her, three sorts of sorbet in a spun-sugar basket – the past flew like a shower of arrows over my head. Only love, you said, makes our lives bearable and without it we scurry for cover like a hunter's prey.

BEFORE NATALIE

12

Ella Waterman Goddard

'Loving is not as easy as it seems.'

In July 1879 Beatrice Romaine Goddard, aged five, stayed at the mansion of her paternal grandfather in Cheshunt Hill, Philadelphia. One night she was woken by screams. Her mad cousin, Mamie Waterman, who was kept locked in rooms at the top of the house, had jumped out of the window. Earlier that day Romaine had called in on her. Deluded that this child was her baby, Mamie opened her bodice, took Romaine on her knee, and pushed her mouth to her breast.

To compound Romaine's terror, her mother, Ella Goddard, told her she had a premonition of this death. She said she hallucinated Mamie crouching behind a chair, then floating through the air and out of the bedroom window.

The Cheshunt Hill estate had twenty acres of gardens, its own farm, woodland and orchards. A seeming paradise of flowers, lawns and hummingbirds, it reflected the fortune Isaac Waterman made from buying mines in Salt Lake City and in Kingston, Pennsylvania. By the terms of his will his money was held in trust to his children with the capital going to his grandchildren.

When she was twenty-four, his daughter Ella, in 1865, married Harry Goddard, an army major. In nine years of marriage they had four children: Katharine, who died after a year; an only son, St Mar, who was as disturbed as his cousin Mamie; Maya, born in 1869; and Beatrice Romaine, born in a Rome hotel on 1 May 1874.

Romaine's parents divorced soon after her birth and her father did not figure in her life. He became an alcoholic and his wife's alimony kept him in drink. Romaine's childhood was ruled by her mother and St Mar and their collusion in madness. Her brother was the focus of her mother's attention. 'She never failed to remind me that I was not good-looking like St Mar, and indeed my pale face and dark hair could in no way compare with his angelic blondness.'

Childhood, she said, was like living on an avalanche: 'no fixity, no foundation, only unfractional time, carrying with it the sensation of danger more mental than physical'. She preferred her mother entirely deranged, talking to herself or to invisible friends. 'She was quite gracious with these phantoms, reserving for this world alone the incessant irritability of her other moods.'

With her children and a retinue of servants, Ella Goddard moved from one hotel and country to another. She made no distinction between day and night, ordered meals at any hour, and seldom slept. She travelled with twenty-two black canvas trunks, fitted with trays that were filled with her possessions. No one knew what was where and a maid would constantly have to unlock them to search unsuccessfully for some item or garment.

Despite the chaos of Ella's life she impressed those in her orbit with a sense of her immense importance. They did her bidding, however bizarre. Rich, arrogant, and elegant, she insisted on being treated with the greatest respect. 'The atmosphere she created was that of a court ruled over by a crazy queen.' Before her son became incurably mad and took all her attention, she treated Romaine either as of royal blood, because she was descended from her, or as a page-in-waiting dressed in her brother's cast-off clothes.

She had a lover when Romaine was four, a shadowy figure known as Mr R, tall and dark, who wrote poems to her. He went with Ella and St Mar on a holiday at Niagara Falls. Romaine stayed behind at Cheshunt Hill with an Irish nurse, Mary O'Neill, who read out letters, taken from her mother's bureau, from Mr R's wife, begging him not to abandon her and his family. Ella returned home subdued: Mr R had leapt into the waterfall. She claimed to have had a premonition of this death too and said he was distressed at being forced to leave her.

After Mr R's suicide, Ella's interest in the occult grew. She subscribed to *Lucifer*,[1] a magazine with a winged devil on its cover, and surrounded herself with paid mediums. Romaine would see them sitting at a table with outstretched hands, waiting for vibrations. Once, when she fell asleep in an adjacent alcove, her mother pulled her awake, shouting 'What did you hear?' and threatening her with a whip. St Mar intervened to protect her. During the seance Ella had had a presentiment of evil; when she caught sight of Romaine slumped in the alcove, she supposed her to be an agent of the devil, and warned her to avert her 'devil's eyes'.

---

1 Published by Madame H.P. Blavatsky between 1885 and 1891, it ran articles about astral bodies or doppelgängers, and the 'Constitution of the Inner Man'.

'It was not long after this that I began watching my mother and my observations became more objective.' As an adult Romaine spoke of herself to Natalie as a martyred child, with her life blighted by her mother's 'mad egotism'. In an unpublished memoir, *No Pleasant Memories*,[2] she said she could not recall a single act of ordinary kindness from her mother whom she distrusted profoundly:

I remember standing before a mirror supporting my mother's arm to ease its weight as she stuck a long pin into her hat, perched high on a structure of curls. The arm was heavy, but I found diversion looking at her image in the mirror. The hand was automatically directing the pin for the raised eyes were fixed far above and beyond the hat, reflecting in their transparency some vision of colourless light. The hand at last fell down, but the eyes remained focused above, unconscious of the moment, unwilling to return. Though this glimpse of my mother's flight into space was fearful in itself, her return to earth could but seem to me even more alarming.

From the age of six, Romaine's way of asserting her identity, and of getting a hold on reality, was to draw. In the many hotels in which she stayed with her mother, sister, and sick brother, she would find a quiet corner, get out pad and pencils and draw the view from the window or remembered images from Cheshunt Hill – cats, trees, and symbols of a kind of home. She hid these drawings in case her mother criticised or destroyed them out of hostility to such displays of individuality.

---

2 Repeated efforts to find a publisher all failed.

A talent to draw was in her control. From an early age she wanted to escape the thrall of madness, break free from her family, and forge a life of her own. But she herself was never to be free from persecutory thoughts, visual hallucinations, and a sense of malign spirits inhabiting the ether. Her form of self-protection was to stay emotionally remote, watchful, guarded, and alone.

10

Aversions are learned. A dud oyster at lunch in a fish restaurant in Essaouria, then an afternoon in the bathroom of room 4 at the Hotel Maroc, taps running to drown my sounds, spraying Bulgari eau de toilette *like Mr Sheen. Dinner cancelled, my birthday treat. Do you like oysters?*

A decade later I tried again. Half a dozen from Whitby Bay, in barnacled shells on a bed of ice, a silver dish, wedges of lemon, a cool accompanying Pouilly Fuissé. I sucked this slithery thing that evoked the ocean, my throat constricted, my stomach heaved.

Then at our mother's hundredth birthday, a private function room at Le Gavroche. Oysters for those who like them, then chicken à la something or maybe duck. We are here because we love you, said Harry with professional sincerity to the frail and gilded star, and I whose life is a careful silence, wearing the rings you gave me, joined the warm applause.

13

St Mar

'Unselfishness may be self-annihilation.'

When he was eleven St Mar had scarlet fever and was sent to Cheshunt Hill to recuperate. After three months there alone with his grandmother, a Jehovah's Witness,[1] he returned to his mother and sisters religiously obsessed. His mental decline was then vivid. He said endless improvised prayers before eating, and thought God and various saints were molesting him. No servant, nurse or barber could get near – he jabbed them with his elbows. His eyes stared and he looked, Romaine said, like 'a fanatic long lost in the desert'.

He was always bizarre and often dangerous. In a disquietingly soft voice he would say he wanted to die. He was afraid to descend hills, went to bed in his overcoat, and would stand by a window tapping the glass and ranting at imagined aggressors. He drank concoctions he had brewed out of leaves and flowers, and threw bottles from high windows on to the heads of pedestrians. When

---

1 Jehovah's Witnesses believe Satan and his Demons pervade the earth tempting all to sin, that Jesus Christ will return to resurrect the righteous dead, and that men are the head of the household.

he did this from a tenth-floor balcony in a Paris hotel the police were called: 'Only the evident state of his mind averted proceedings against him.' He rode a tricycle, muffled in his overcoat and oblivious of traffic. One day in Windsor he returned to the hotel muddy and with his coat torn. A coachman had told him he should ride on the left: he had refused and the man had hit him. His tricycle was taken from him and he went to bed inveighing against the English.

Ella paid for a Dr Phillips to accompany them as they roamed from Nice to Paris, London, or New York. Alexander Hamilton Phillips was young and tubercular, with spurious qualifications, but he had a talent, in Ella's view, to evoke spirits at her seances. St Mar hated him.

They travelled in intense confusion with Ella's trunks lost, or St Mar refusing to get out of the train when they arrived at some destination. When Phillips dragged him to the platform, St Mar would hit him or make a scene. Phillips would then snap the end off a glass ampoule of ether, empty it onto a pad of cotton wool, and press it to St Mar's nose.

Ella called St Mar her darling boy and her beautiful St Amar. He responded to such endearments by prodding her toes with a cane. When she took no notice, he persisted. When she gave him a clock of crystal and gold that told the days of the week, the tides of the moon, and changes in the weather, he smashed it. 'No Christian,' he said, 'could accept a clock which began the week on a Saturday.'

Romaine stayed up at night with him playing cards, but never allowed herself the doubtful privilege of winning.

Had I done so it would have meant to my brother a defeat beyond cards or a game of the moment. In some inarticulate and immature way I surveyed rather than lived my life, never supposing that I really belonged either to my mother or my brother. I pitied my brother. My mother I first feared, then watched, then judged.

As for her sister Maya, Romaine made no reference to her. It was as if she did not exist.[2]

Ella spent thousands of dollars on attempted cures for St Mar. In 1881 he returned from a clinic in New York more ill than ever. Romaine said her mother then punished her for being in good health while St Mar was incurable. 'Looking back on this time it is hard to make allowance for the many miseries I had to endure.' She said her mother's 'maleficence' peaked when she dragged her into a room, pulled off her velvet jacket, chopped off all her hair, then told her Irish washerwoman, Mrs Hickey, to look after her, saying she could not cope.

Mrs Hickey lived at the top of a tenement building on Third Avenue. She took Romaine there by tram, gave her bread, butter and a large cup of black coffee, the sofa to sleep on, pencils and paper to draw with, and a cupboard to keep them in. She introduced her to neighbours: a young man who drew copies of photographs, his mother who knitted woollen hats, a woman who painted extravagant seascapes and framed them in velvet. Romaine was free to play in the street, roller skate, and meet other children. She said she felt superior to them and that they called her saucer eyes.

2 Maya's true name was Mary Aimée. She was two years older than Romaine, but they looked very similar.

When she got lost, a policeman brought her back to Mrs Hickey.

Each week Mrs Hickey took Ella's ironed washing to her. She cried on the day she found Ella had disappeared, leaving neither an address nor money for the washing or child care. No one knew where Ella had gone. Romaine went hungry, fetched water in a pitcher from the public pump, sold newspapers for dimes, drew and painted, slept in the same room as the beer-drinking Mrs Hickey and declined the butcher's invitation to adopt her.

All of which, she said, was preferable to life with mother. Then one day, in the timeless hinterland of her childhood, Mr Barr, her grandfather's secretary arrived. He gave Mrs Hickey a wad of notes and took Romaine to Cheshunt Hill for a summer of freedom, good food and fine clothes. But, Romaine wrote in her memoir, beneath this unexpected happiness she was aware of 'a secret craving for the negative exultation of those who are solitary and adrift'.

In autumn 1884 she was boarded at St Catherine's Hall, an Episcopal Church School in New Jersey – a repressive place of stiff muslin, no games or raised voices, and a great deal of thanking God. The headmaster took to drink when his wife died, gave incomprehensible Bible readings and called the senior girls into his study to kiss them. Romaine received long religious letters from her grandmother and was belatedly baptised without her mother's consent. She said the only friend she made was a hunchbacked blonde girl who reminded her of St Mar.

Once her father visited. He gave her a box of caramels, commended her drawings and said he admired the illustrations of Gustave Doré.[3] Romaine disliked his drooping moustache.

---

3 Gustave Doré (1832–83), French book illustrator and painter, whose works include engravings for *London: A pilgrimage* (1872), *Perrault's Fairy Tales*, and the Bible.

'Belonging to one parent was a disagreeable experience. I had no desire to belong to another.'

She had recurring visual hallucinations. She was told of two former pupils from Egypt who had died at the school – one of fever, the other supposedly of grief. At night she saw the backs of these phantom girls. She thought they watched her every movement and she willed herself to ignore them.

She told no one of the crushes she had on older girls, which even to herself were incoherent. Her schoolwork was average, her drawing exceptional, and she won a gold pen as a prize for calligraphy. At the end of her fourth year, when she was thirteen, Dr Phillips was sent to collect her to rejoin her mother, brother, and sister in London at the Hotel De Keyser: 'As I greeted my mother and recognized the same mad luminous eyes and unsmiling mouth, I felt the apprehension of a small animal caught in a net and for no good of its own. Had it been possible I would have left then and there.'

St Mar, who was nineteen, wore black velvet: he was thin and stooped, his tangled blond hair merged with an uncut beard and he peered at Romaine through his fingers. He had a valet whom he hated. Ella's maid was frightened of her, and a governess, hired for Romaine, left after trying unsuccessfully to make her memorise a list of Saxon kings.

Romaine entered again into her mother's confusion of purposeless moving, structureless days and obscure soliloquies. After a year of it she was at the point of breakdown. 'St Mar's pale face loomed, my mother's wild eyes gleamed like evil beacons. A very little more and this nether world would have held me altogether.' In a Florence hotel room she tried to kill herself by swallowing the sulphur heads of matches.

11

I opened the cupboard in the private room off Kipperton Ward. In it was a black box. I asked mother what it was. She did not answer. I examined cursorily its live and neutral wires, its plugs and headpieces, connections, dials and calibration devices. It was a machine for administering electro-convulsions. It looked like a device for kick-starting a flat battery. Something to do with garages and car parts.

14

The Artist

'I am most curious about myself.'

After her suicide display, Romaine was sent to a convent near Genoa. 'I was left there to adapt myself as best I could to a life of medieval Catholicism.' The school, a high-walled, grey-stone building with unheated classrooms and dormitories, was like a prison, the food was monotonous – beetroot salad, tuna and cheese – she was the only English-speaking girl there, and she struggled to understand the lessons which were either in Latin or Italian.

Her sense of being martyred grew. Other girls went home at weekends and got hampers at Christmas. The uniform was a check dress that covered her neck and wrists and reached to her ankles, her hair was wound into a plaited bun at the nape of her neck, washing was discouraged because of its sensual edge and there were no mirrors.

For consolation she kept in a pocket a photograph of one of the nuns she thought beautiful – Sister Marcia on her deathbed; she had died of a tooth infection. When Romaine was ill with pneumonia her mother visited and brought her a gold coin and a photograph of herself to replace the one of Sister Marcia. The nuns pushed relics and images of saints under her pillow and gave her *Addio al Protestantismo* to read and Queen Victoria's Diary while on a visit to the Highlands.

Romaine's ability to draw was encouraged. From images in psalters and prayer books, she drew a life-sized head of Christ crowned with thorns, angels on tombs, and doleful virgins. She was told that were she to be accepted into the sisterhood, she would be the drawing teacher.

But she was too rejecting of orthodoxies, too odd and rebellious ever to satisfy the convent nuns. After four years she was expelled for recalcitrance. She had called a nun blue-nosed and refused to genuflect before an ivory image of the crucified Christ. Nor would she place her rosary on the glass case containing the preserved body of a saint. Sister Cecilia told her that a bad Protestant could not make a good Catholic and that she would write a letter to her mother informing her of her expulsion. Again Dr Phillips came to collect Romaine. One of the girls, Armine, gave her a bunch of flowers as she left.

While Romaine was interned in her convent, Ella had developed a passion for acquiring property. She owned six apartments in Nice alone. In the hope that St Mar would benefit from a permanent home, she bought the Château Grimaldi in nearby Menton. In its terraced grounds, that stretched down to the Mediterranean, she had designed palm-shaded walks, rock gardens, and beds of exotic flowers. The house had thirty rooms on four floors, which she filled with chandeliers, exotic carpets, marble statues, Oriental draperies, and furniture adorned with angels and gilt flowers. The library ceiling was painted with cupids holding up the world on which was gilded ELLA in large letters. Among the books that lined its walls was Immanuel Kant's *Critique of Pure Reason*,[1] in which she had written a dedication to St Mar.

Ella occupied one half of the house, St Mar the other in rooms decorated in gold with garlands of flowers twisted round pink columns. Romaine was given rooms on the top floor. The setting was ornate, but the psychodrama was the same. The house was heavily curtained against the sun with blocks of ice to cool the rooms. Ella reclined on a couch and gave unpredictable commands while servants fanned her. St Mar liked to pound on a piano. Ella believed him to be a genius and summoned Romaine to marvel at the cacophony he made. Romaine felt herself to be as strange as them both: 'I fought hard to keep in contact with the sunny outer world, but my efforts were in vain.' One night, woken by the smell of burning, she found St Mar naked, setting fire to his nightshirt with a candle. He said the Invisible had worn it so he had to destroy it.

In autumn 1891 Ella and St Mar went to England and Romaine was sent to Mademoiselle Bertin's Private Finishing School for Young Ladies in Geneva, where rich girls of many nationalities were taught how to manage the servants, place guests at dinner, and defer to their husbands.

Romaine was seventeen. She ignored the curriculum. She had plenty of time, she said, to draw sad, drooping figures under equally drooping willow trees, or Death and the Devil rocking the cradles of doomed infants. 'I still possess a drawing of this last subject.' And girls desired her: Karina called her Don Juan, and wrote of

---

1 First published in 1781, it has chapters on transcendental logic, space, time, and the discipline of pure reason.

holding her hand and kissing her pretty red lips; Hélène, a Greek
redhead with a prodigious memory for celebrities, liked to look
into her eyes and cuddle close, until they were forbidden to be
alone together in each other's rooms.

Romaine's interests defined as art, music and girls. Her mother
agreed that after a year at finishing school she could study singing
and French in Paris. From the Paris paper *Galignani*,[2] Ella found
a family in Neuilly, a Monsieur and Madame Givend, who offered
lodgings to musical young ladies. Their house was small and dingy,
Romaine's room was cold, and at mealtimes Toto the dog rooted
in the dishes on the dinner table. Louise Givend, their only daughter,
had a secret lover and curvature of the spine. She made her own
underwear trimmed with yellow lace and showed Romaine pornog-
raphy printed and published in Belgium and Holland. Romaine
saw plenty of 'photographic variations on the sexual act'.

These living quarters seemed as inimical to her as Mrs Hickey's in
New York, or the Italian convent, until another lodger arrived. Clara
Butt,[3] who was six foot two and sang *Home Sweet Home* to Romaine,
was in Paris to study with Jacques Bouhy.[4] She had already sung the
title role in Gluck's *Orfeo ed Euridice* at the Lyceum Theatre in London.
Her voice ranged from below middle C to high B flat. 'My life was
transformed,' Romaine wrote. 'I now lived on a higher plane of love
and adoration. My new friend radiated kindness and sympathy.'

---

2 Giovanni Antonio Galignani (1752–1821), born in Brescia, went to Paris and from 1814
 published *Galignani's Messenger*, a daily paper in English. In 1904 it became the *Daily
 Messenger*.

3 Clara Butt (1872–1936), English contralto. Her repertoire included Bach, Handel and
 popular ballads. Her renditions of 'There is no death' and 'Abide with me' brought the
 house down. Elgar's *Sea Pictures* was written for her.

4 Jacques Bouhy also taught the English contralto Louise Kirkby-Lunn, a student of
 Radclyffe Hall's stepfather, Alberto Visetti.

She liked to sit in Clara Butt's room, holding hands and kissing. Madame Givend complained about such unnatural goings-on in her house. Romaine said of herself that she did not care about vice and virtue as defined by religion or society and that her reference was solely to her own emotions and aesthetic sensibility.

When Clara Butt left the Givends', Romaine was desolate. She made a decision to go her own way without telling her mother. She packed her suitcases when the Givends were out and with the 1,000 francs she had saved, rented a garret in the eighteenth arrondissement in the Avenue de Clichy. She earned a little as an artist's model: an Englishman painted her languishing on the banks of the Seine, gave her tea and cakes, and warned that such independence would end in prostitution. Undeterred she bought a bicycle and rode at night in the Bois de Boulogne with red Japanese lanterns dangling from her handlebars.

She was tall and slim, her eyes and hair were dark and she was alone in Paris. She, too, had leisure to exchange long looks and half-smiles with strangers in the Avenue des Acacias and in the rue de Seine. Often she was propositioned. On a day when she stopped for lemonade at the Pavillon Chinois, a well-dressed woman came and sat at her table. Her eyes 'dazzled', Romaine said. She invited Romaine for a drive in her carriage. A woman at another table threw a carafe of water at Romaine and left the café. Like Natalie, Romaine went with her perfect stranger to the Palais de Glace. Like Natalie, she spent the afternoon at the woman's apartment. But for Romaine it was not a joyous encounter, or a quest for love. She had no theories about Sappho or the island of Lesbos, nor did she have an ambition to live her life as a work of art. Sex for her was an impulsive act and she did not feel comfortable in anyone's company for long.

12

On a rainy morning in a near-empty café I had a cappuccino and a croissant. A stranger with grey eyes asked if she might sit at my table. In a way I thought I knew her, that I had been waiting there for her. We talked of the rain, of the sculptures she made, of our love and hatred of the city. I looked at her hands. She gave me her phone number on a scrap of paper. I have it to this day in a file marked Personal.

15

The Doctors

*'Her hate moves under her words like beetles
under a stone disturbed.'*

Romaine's freedom depended on her mother's money. Ella was prepared to send her an allowance but in return wanted to exert control. She liked, when it suited her, to send details of St Mar's and her own symptoms and travels, and for Romaine to visit and say what she was doing. She always enclosed money with her letters and would send clothes: silk dresses embroidered with lace, a warm Astrakhan tippet[1] and muff, flannel knickers, wool gloves, a plush winter jacket. She said she did not mind if 'an occasional young gentleman' called on Romaine. 'I want you to act "straight" with me,' she wrote.

Romaine dreaded receiving letters from her. They held a madness of syntax and content, a meandering warning, an incipient paranoia and were worse than disconcerting to receive:

---

1 A sort of scarf, headdress, or cape.

Jan 5 1894 Poste Restante Algiers
My dear Beatrice

Self-assumption & assertion in social life is very *under*-bred – and
when those useful folk take their hand off the plough of fallow
ground & want to teach the waves how to roll & rule the stars in
their courses – it is very comical. Declaration, & ranting, are quite
interesting accomplishments sometimes however – although not
very practical – it was said that the great Mrs Siddons would ask
for a 'pot o' beer' so tragically that the waiter would fairly leap into
the air. But I think you like a role occasionally – do you not my
dear. I saw before leaving however you were beginning something
'crooked' and I would have removed you had I the time. They were
playing their little games off on you – and you were inflating &
giving one or two to me second-hand – like a dear foolish little
monkey, & soon were grinding me out like a coffee mill – Why
– when I am interesting myself – in spite of St Mar's sickness –
why do you throw cold water on me – by impatience – and even
by a spirit of dictation – which is absurd – but I suppose you do
not realize it. You seemed inclined to turn your nose up at everything I began. Can you not see that there are times when, as you
are doing nothing to help – the least is to try not to worry at me.
Well – I won't scold – but it seems a pity that you are often so
resentful of advice or restraint from your mother whom you could
accept it from – in an attentive & pleasant spirit without humiliation – and by whose side you might have advantages – otherwise impossible to me – as you can comprehend. I do not suppose
you are so stupid as not to understand her superiority – not only
in the social advantages – but in so many more mental – to those

employed – of course I do not occupy myself with the details of 'tuning up' but on account of all this sickness I have been more reserved than necessary – but it is I am the only '*chef d'orchestre*'.

And pages more in similar vein. To avoid receiving such letters, Romaine asked her brother's doctor, Alexander Phillips, to intercede and arrange for an allowance to be sent to her direct from her grandfather's solicitors in America. Phillips visited her in Paris. She did not know that with an eye to his own financial future he had proposed to Ella Goddard and been spurned.

On Romaine's behalf he wrote to the executors of the family trust. A reply came from her mother. It was rational but discouraging:

The letter you sent to America was forwarded to me. I wish you to understand that my executors have no authority to pay out my money to you or to anyone without my consent. Considering the manner in which you ran away you have nullified even a right to consanguinity. I am much amused at your logic – to earn your own living independently of me and yet ask for my money to do so. However, as I know it is not so easy to set the Thames on fire as you had supposed, I enclose Frs 300 – which you must promptly acknowledge to me – particularly if you wish me to assist you in the future.

Romaine was to need future assistance. She had had sex with Phillips which left her pregnant. She was drawn to him, though she recoiled from his protruding eyes, thin blond hair and receding chin. He was part of the family caprice and melodrama. He had observed the madness of her mother and brother, and had seemed like a friend when he collected her from schools in New Jersey and Genoa.

After proposing to Ella and seducing Romaine, Phillips eloped to New York with Maya, Romaine's enigmatic elder sister. They married in the Little Church Around the Corner[2] and within two years had two daughters, Ella Beatrice and Liliane. The marriage was unworkable until Ella provided an allowance and took the elder girl to live with her. Phillips died seven years later at the age of forty-four. Maya then moved to the Château Grimaldi and married the Comte de Valbranca, a despotic Italian diplomat of extreme right-wing views.[3]

Ella sent Romaine a basic monthly allowance of 300 francs. It was enough to survive. For extra money Romaine sang in a *café-chantant* wearing a poke bonnet and a wig of yellow curls, a job she lost when she refused to dance a jig. She was isolated: 'I knew nothing about friends and my newly acquired independence absorbed me entirely.'

Through a *bureau de location* she found remote country lodgings where she could secretly give birth to the child. True to the ghoulish backdrop to her life, she lodged with a couple whom she believed had murdered two of their children. No one knew where she was and each day she walked alone in the forest. She said that the only other lodger was a veiled woman covered in sores who

---

2 On East 29th Street, between Fifth and Madison Avenues, known also as the Church of Transfiguration.

3 He spied on her and opened her letters. They sold the château to Dr Serge Voronoff, who conducted experiments on the sex glands of the monkeys he kept caged in the grounds.

sat all day crying and kissing a photograph, and the floor of whose room was strewn with wads of blood-soaked cotton. Romaine had a daughter whom she gave to a convent. Five years later she learned that the baby had died aged two and a half months.

Her mother, who knew nothing of this drama, in 1878 married Phillips' successor, Dr George Crampton, thirty years her junior and the son of a Rock Island bookseller. Like Alice Barney, Ella chose a young man to control and flaunt. For her trousseau she bought silk underwear fringed with lace butterflies and had ELLA embroidered on her silk sheets. They honeymooned on a boat to Genoa with St Mar who kept threatening to kill this stepfather.

A year passed before Crampton fled, saying he had been ill-treated. He refused to return, so Ella filed for divorce on the grounds of desertion. A maid at the Château Grimaldi spoke of the terrible life he had led and how his wife humiliated him.

Romaine described her family life as a twilight world peopled with shadowy strangers in malevolent pursuit, orchestrated by her mother's darkness and unreason. It held palpable menace. She determined to 'hold the ancestral passions in leash', sever all contact with her mother, stay true to her own talent, and 'obey no other urge than that of my art, even though it might lead to the depths of mental distress'.

She kept her mother's letters from Paris, Nice, Algiers, and New York as testimony to her own ordeal. Her mother rebuked her for not writing more often and for scorning all effort she made. 'You can very well take a little trouble to write – even if it is not a pleasure to you.' She tried to tell Romaine of her concerns for St Mar and his constant suffering, of her fear that he would die, of how she stayed up day and night caring for him, and how discouraging it all was. She said that when Romaine was hostile towards her, she reacted by being more exacting and indifferent than she wanted to be.

When Romaine cut herself off from her, her mother turned on her, called her thankless, perverse and impatient, a law unto herself, 'and a law unto her betters sometimes'. Her daughter became one more person who abandoned her.

13

I hurry home to you. I push open the door, the shopping is heavy, you put food in the fridge, fruit in a bowl, I get a vase for the flowers and uncork the wine. Your eyes look happy. We talk of a trip to the Creole coral reefs of Cahuita. Just for a while I feel safe and arrived.

16

Rome and Capri

'Work up the brute circumstance that life throws at us,
and remake it in our own image.'

Romaine thought her singing voice too cold and ecclesiastical to pursue music as a career. She decided to study art, and in October 1898 bought a third-class train ticket and travelled to Rome with a small suitcase and a pearl-handled pistol.

She booked into a hotel and looked for rooms to rent. When the manager propositioned her she threatened to shoot him. She found a ground-floor studio in the Via Sistina, but again was harassed by the landlord who hinted he would climb through her window at night. She threatened to shoot him too, and slept with the window closed.

She enrolled for the life class at La Scuola Nazionale and ate at the Caffè Greco, a students' café in the Via Condotti. Tuition was free but it troubled her that all the other students and the model were male. Each evening she went to another drawing class at the Circolo Artistico where she was one of four women in a class of thirty. A bearded Sicilian left 'disgusting picture cards' on her chair. The third time he did this, she slapped his face. Fearing retaliation, she then stayed away from the school. 'No Sicilian accepts a slap from a woman,' she said. Though asked by a tutor to return, she refused, and instead drew alone in museums using statues as models.

As ever she felt herself to be outside the social group in which she moved. She called herself a *lapidé*, 'stoned to death' and martyred by Philistines. She saw herself as the melancholy artist, living on a pittance and in service to a wider truth.

'I had always stood alone and would proudly continue to do so,' she wrote. 'Who within the despised circle had ever come forward to help me? The rich relations, who now held aloof from the unavoidable break with my mother, had never raised a voice on my behalf.'

She did not, like Natalie, feel defined as lesbian. Rather she felt kinship with homosexual men. She befriended John Fothergill,[1] an Oxford graduate, and together they visited galleries and monuments in Rome, and travelled to Assisi to look at paintings by Giotto.[2] At school Fothergill had kept an image of the marble head of a Greek boy in the same way that Romaine had kept a photograph of a nun. He admired Oscar Wilde and knew Alfred Douglas. Though repelled by girls, he thought Romaine's face 'open like a boy's'. She painted a portrait of his head and shoulders, a conventional piece without the austere quality of the style she was to find.

She could not walk the city without being importuned and she

---

1 John Rowland Fothergill (1876–1957). In the 1920s he became an innkeeper and bought the Spreadeagle in Thame, the Royal Hotel in Ascot and the Three Swans in Market Harborough. He wrote *An Innkeeper's Diary, Confessions of an Innkeeper* and *My Three Inns*. The Spreadeagle was one of Evelyn Waugh's favourite eateries. He inscribed a copy of *Decline and Fall* with 'To John Fothergill, Oxford's only civilising influence'. In *Brideshead Revisited* Anthony Blanche takes Charles Ryder to the Spreadeagle. Fothergill married and had two sons.
2 Giotto di Bondone (1267–1337). St Francis of Assisi is buried in the Basilica where Giotto painted frescoes of his life.

became afraid. At the Circolo she posed for a student who assumed she would have sex with him. On impulse when summer came she left Rome. 'Someone had spoken to me of Capri and it was there I decided to go.' She had heard of the ease and safety of its artists' community and of the beauty of the island: the light, the hills, dusty paths that ran between old stone walls and oleander trees, vineyards and orange groves, the sea, and Vesuvius looming in the distance.

It took two hours by steamer from Naples. Many English-speaking artists and writers settled or summered in Capri. There was an atmosphere of acceptance and serenity; food and rents were cheap, and wine plentiful. Romaine found a chapel with high Gothic windows for her studio. It had a red-brick floor, niches in the stone walls, and an arch that led to a courtyard of fig trees. She acquired an iron washstand, an easel, ten books and a dog called Marco. She breakfasted in her shaded garden before the sun was hot, swam in the sea at the Bagno Timberino, called at the post office for letters and papers brought by the midday steamer, and welcomed the island's peace.

But for some months she could not work. 'What had my predilection for the sad and grey to do with the sharp Capri sunlight and blue shadows?' She would plant her easel in some isolated place, then sit in front of it doing nothing. At night she heard the sound of strange birds that no one else could hear.

'Among all the colony,' the novelist E.F. Benson[3] wrote of those

---

3 Edward Frederic Benson (1867–1940), English novelist, best known for his six Mapp and Lucia comic novels, published in the 1930s and set in Rye. He was a friend of Radclyffe Hall and Una Troubridge. Una thought he had never been in love with a man, 'just fond'. None of his five brothers and sister married. He told Una how when his brother Hugh, a Catholic prelate, died, he left a box containing a 'discipline' – a scourge of small spikes stuck with congealed blood.

on Capri, 'I cannot recall one who could be called ordinary.' Romaine was free to be a *lapidé* in safe and beautiful surroundings, with uncensorious neighbours.

Axel Munthe lived at Anacapri in his villa, San Michele,[4] with its cypresses, garlands of vines and marble statues of gods. Compton Mackenzie had a villa on the southern slopes of Monte Solaro. Somerset Maugham[5] spent a summer on the island when he was twenty-three, after the success in 1897 of his first novel, *Liza of Lambeth* and had his first homosexual affair there with another Englishman, John Ellingham Brooks, whose life's work was to translate Heredia's sonnets from Greek to English.

At the Grande Marina, in a white house with floors of Moorish tiles and loggias with trellised roofs covered in vines, lived Kate and Sadie Perry, two elderly American sisters. They travelled the world collecting paintings, oriental rugs, and Chinese porcelain. In their garden on Sunday afternoons, in a circular marble 'Temple of Vesta', their cultured expatriate friends were served caviar sandwiches, ices, sugar cakes, cigars and an alcoholic brew with strawberries floating in it. The talk was of art and literature. John Brooks was a favoured guest, another was Count Fersen who smoked opium, wore embroidered robes and liked sex with boys. The sisters took him with them on tours of India and China.

---

4 Axel Munthe (1857–1949), Swedish physician and writer, whose autobiography *The Story of San Michele* (1929) was about his work as a doctor in Paris, Rome and Capri. He financed sanctuaries for migrating birds on Capri and in Sweden, and gave to charities for the poor.

5 Somerset Maugham (1874–1965), British novelist and playwright, born in the British Embassy in Paris. For ten years, while Maugham was married to the interior designer Syrie Wellcome, his lover was the American, Gerald Haxton. Syrie divorced Maugham: Haxton was deported from Britain, and went to live with Maugham in his villa at Cap Ferrat on the Côte d'Azure.

'Art for art's sake was the only thing that mattered in the world, and the artist alone gave this ridiculous world significance,' Somerset Maugham wrote of the Capri colony. Charles Coleman, an American, painted rugged fishermen and pale pink and blue pictures of Vesuvius. Mrs Kennedy Fraser, a Scottish composer, spent her mornings in the sea, wore a tartan skirt, and would stand on a chair to sing 'Auld Lang Syne'.[6] In the evenings everyone met at Morgano's Bar, off the Piazza, to drink and talk.

Romaine found freedom, ease, and sunshine. A charcoal self-portrait, done at this time, shows her with hair loose and in casual clothes. She sold such work as she produced. Thomas Burr, an American author, commissioned his portrait for 500 lire; Romaine bought a table, desk, and chair with the money. James Whipple, an English explorer, bought a painting by her of a Capri child holding a bunch of berries, then offered 2,000 lire for a portrait of himself. In his villa in Anacapri he posed in khaki, with leather boots, sitting on a campstool with a cane across his knees. He, too, tried to kiss her and squash her against the wall so she left with the portrait unfinished.

Her picture of a sunny pergola with green vines and purple

6 A traditional Scottish song penned by Robert Burns (1759–96). He wrote it down from hearing an old man singing the original Jacobite version:

> Should auld acquaintance be forgot,
> And never brought to mind?
> Should auld acquaintance be forgot
> And days of auld lang syne?
> And days of auld lang syne, my dear
> And days of auld lang syne,
> Should auld acquaintance be forgot
> And days of auld lang syne?

'Auld lang syne' appears to mean 'old long ago' in Scots.

grapes was bought by the American art collector Charles Freer.[7] She complained to him that she was dissatisfied and without true friends, and that the sociability of the place was anathema to her. She had, she said, no desire to marry, nor did she think herself wise, or a good painter.

He advised her to study further; on his recommendation she kept her studio in Capri and enrolled in 1900 for a term at the Académie Colarossi in Paris to work at portrait painting. Freer took her to dinner and to a variety show in Paris, invited her to London and, like the others, propositioned her.

She seemed as unsettled as her mother, unable to stay long anywhere and unfocused in her work. She returned to Capri wanting its distinctive charm but not knowing what to paint. And then, soon after Christmas 1901, when she collected her post and papers she saw an announcement in the *New York Herald*: 'Mr St Amar Goddard, the brilliant son of Mrs Ella Waterman Goddard and Major Henry Goddard, has died at Nice of an illness that cut short a promising career.' A letter followed from her mother requesting help. Mr Whipple agreed to look after Marco the dog but as payment asked for a goodbye kiss. 'As I ungraciously offered my cheek I could not help thinking how unpleasant such a perfunctory gesture can be.'

---

7 Charles Lang Freer (1856–1919) made money from the American railroads, then from 1900 for the rest of his life collected art. He left his entire collection and the building that houses it – designed by him – to the Smithsonian Institute in Washington.

14

My erstwhile partner Gwen, St Gwen you called her, after parting from me soon found Gina — at a Hammersmith meeting of lesbian doctors. She inseminated her with the sperm of Daniel, a gay nurse in a committed relationship with Richard, a psychotherapist. Their four-year-old, Johnnie, has bright eyes, curly hair, two mummies and daddies and a surfeit of toys. Gwen and Gina run an orderly home with a well-stocked deep-freeze, a nanny, and full diaries. Anniversaries are remembered, there is shared money in the bank, and the contented cat, called Sweetie Pie, is from a rescue home.

17

More Ella Waterman Goddard

'Our shadows are taller than ourselves.'

Ella Goddard looked ill and mad. She was untidily dressed in black with a blonde wig that tipped to one side and showed wispy grey hair. Romaine was eerily fascinated to see her after five years. They stayed together in the Nice apartment in which St Mar had died. Maya was at the Château Grimaldi with her daughters.

Ella had turned St Mar's bedroom into a mortuary chamber and shrine. On the walls were photographs framed in black of his corpse, on a bier were flowers, under a glass cover were his death-bed and a cast of his right hand. Around the room were facing pairs of his death mask. Ella called these a duality in death whose purpose was to help him journey to an astral sphere.

On guard at the door to the room was a stout man in frock coat and tails, with a heavily made-up face. He called himself Count Louis Hamon,[1] palmist, occultist, and clairvoyant. He had

---

1 Count Hamon (1866–1936) was born William John Warner in Dublin. His clients included Oscar Wilde, Mata Hari, and Sarah Bernhardt. He was the author of *When Were You Born?*, *The Language of the Hand*, *Cheiro's Palmistry*, and *Cheiro's World Predictions*.

published books about his predictions, which included the death of Rasputin[2] and the end of the world. Ella had hired him to keep her in touch with St Mar on his heavenly journeys. Like other of her employees he hoped to marry her for her money.

She railed against the Riviera that had played her false by not bringing St Mar health. She had wanted to bury him in a mausoleum in the grounds of the Château Grimaldi, but this needed permission from the regional authorities, which was not forthcoming, so he had been interned in a vault in the leafy Russian cemetery in Caucade, near Nice. His coffin had a glass panel so that his dead, waxy face could be viewed. Ella took Romaine to see him, and walked behind their carriage as though it were a hearse.

Most of Ella's servants had left. At dinner a place was laid at table for St Mar. Ella said the cutlery jingled because of his presence. At night Romaine felt afraid to sleep in case of surprise attack from her mother. There was no lock on her bedroom door so she looped lengths of string from the bed to the door handle and balanced a log of wood that would fall and wake her if the door opened.

In her preoccupation with St Mar, Ella had neglected her own health. Her symptoms were vomiting, weight loss, extravagant thirst, and itching skin. A small scratch would become infected. Her doctors had assumed all her problems to be mental but she had untreated diabetes and was mortally ill. Romaine tried to supervise her medical care, but her mother resented her. 'She knew that she was dying and I alive watching. I wondered if her hate could die with death or if it might always hover over me.'

---

2   Grigory Yefimovich Rasputin (1871–1916), Russian miracle worker, murdered by Prince Felix Felixovich Yusupov, cousin of Tsar Nicholas II.

Ella became deluded and paranoid, and in pain from an infected arm. On the morning of the day she died she asked to be taken to St Mar's room. At its door she said some object was barring her entry. Romaine pretended to push it aside. Her mother lay on a divan in the room and talked to St Mar's relics. Servants then carried her back to her bed. Some hours later, Romaine said, while a dog howled in the garden, her mother clawed the sheets, asked in an incoherent way for Romaine to forgive her, said, 'It is so cold, so cold,' and died.

Her body was wrapped in white and lighted candles were placed round it. Romaine did not kiss her and as always felt like a spectator: 'I felt no grief. My mother was only a phenomenon I had been watching fearfully all my life. Death the climax nothing more.' That night Romaine woke in a sweat to sounds of thudding on the bathroom door and said she knew it was her mother.

Count Hamon left for Paris and other engagements. Romaine, afraid to stay in the apartment, which she considered haunted, booked in at the Hôtel d'Angleterre on the Promenade des Anglais in a room that looked out over the sea. She wanted anonymity and the reassuring sounds of the ocean, but in the night felt the same terror and heard the same thumps:

During that visit from my mother and the many others that were to follow, though I was frozen, my mind through force of will kept its balance. In time I ceased to hear those ghostly sounds. Yet I was always conscious that there was still a haunting presence which inspired fear, though it eluded even the abstractions of a dream.

Less abstract was the huge inheritance that came her way. Between them, she and her sister benefited from the six apartments in Nice, another in Monte Carlo, one in Dieppe, an unfurnished one in Paris, the Château Grimaldi, and a share of the capital accrued by their grandfather. An American cousin, who directed the estate, wired money to settle Ella's affairs. Romaine disposed of her mother's clothes, furs, linens and lace, dozens of death masks of St Mar packed in straw, a trunk of wigs, another of false teeth. Among the paintings sold was one of a dark, mysterious woman holding a piece of tulle over her breasts. 'I was told that this was supposed to be a portrait of me, the daughter of the house, who had fled home to take refuge in a convent.'

Romaine stayed in the south of France until the will was probated and all property sold. For those months she moved into St Mar's rooms at the Château Grimaldi. She had the walls papered in grey, brought in plain oak furniture and ordered tailored coats and skirts for herself from Redfern Outfitters.

Despite such assertions of identity she still heard St Mar's distressed voice calling her, and what she supposed to be the sounds of her mother's body falling from a bed. She was sure a fire in one of the empty flats had been started by her mother's ghost. She had a recurring nightmare of a genderless figure, with a pale round face and wisps of black hair, that towered over her and tried to lure her into a forest cave. 'I fled through labyrinths of trees, the roots holding me back, the dampness sucking me to earth.'

She wandered the hills of Menton and felt that she was becoming as unstable as her mother and brother. She resolved to get away and to paint again. She bought a life-size lay figure[3] and had a box made especially for it: 'It symbolised years of longing for the unobtainable.' Although it was like a corpse in a coffin waiting for resurrection and she never drew from it, the figure in the box travelled with her and informed the style of bleak portraiture she was soon to find – as did her mother and brother whose presence remained with her like the spectre of death.

---

3 A dummy in the form of an artist's jointed model of the human figure.

18

John Ellingham Brooks

'It is time for dead languages to be quiet.'

Romaine returned to Capri in spring 1903, transformed by wealth: 'I knew that the monastic life so congenial to me was now over.' With a flourish she gave a wad of banknotes to the island's beggar, who skipped round her courtyard chanting 'Viva la Signorina Romana'. But her main beneficiary was John Ellingham Brooks, whose translation of Heredia's sonnets was proceeding slowly.

Brooks was short, pipe-smoking, handsome and homosexual. As a young man, he had gone from England to Capri for a holiday and stayed, liking its beauty and quasi-artistic life. Romaine said he passed hours each day swaying on a piano stool playing Beethoven's Waldstein Sonata with an amateur's skill.

His piano was out of tune, he lived in a neglected villa and his dogs were covered in ticks. In Italian he read Leopardi,[1] Dante[2]

---

[1] Giacomo Leopardi (1798–1837), Italian elegiac poet.
[2] Dante Alighieri (1265–1321), Italian allegorical poet, author of *The Divine Comedy*, chronicler of the middle ages.

and D'Annunzio and he extolled the writing of Meredith[3] and Walter Pater.[4] At his suggestion, Romaine, now she was rich, bought Pater's complete works bound in leather.

She married Brooks on 13 June. Like all her moves it was impulsive, but she hoped they might share a cultured life and that he would encourage her work and protect her from importunate men. She also wanted to change her name so as to escape the thrall of her mother and brother. He wanted an income, and his debts paid. She wrote one word in her diary, 'Married'.

Brooks soon became proprietorial and critical of her appearance and behaviour. In the expectation that together they would go on a walking tour of England she bought a sketchbook, knapsack, and casual clothes and had her hair cut short. Brooks said he felt compromised being seen with her, looking as she did. 'So there was to be no walking tour with knapsack and sketchbook, no help in my efforts to escape the conventional. I could but choose to face the future alone.'

Within weeks she could not tolerate his company. She disliked his habits and manners, his boyfriends, the smell of his tobacco. Worse, he talked as if her money was his too and suggested she make a will, 'in case something happened to her'. The suggestion galvanised her: 'Now something was indeed happening to me.' Disinclined to confront him, she told him she was going to visit London and would meet him there.

---

3 George Meredith (1828–1909), English novelist and poet, author of *The Shaving of Shagpat*, *The Egoist*, and *Diana of the Crossways*.

4 Walter Horatio Pater (1839–94), English essayist, critic and Oxford don, extolled art as the true religion, was tutor to and friend of Oscar Wilde, and wrote *Marius the Epicurean*, a model of the aesthetic hero.

She bought a house with a large studio in Tite Street, Chelsea. Oscar Wilde had lived in Tite Street in 1884, Whistler had worked there, until he died in 1903, and John Singer Sargent[5] had a studio opposite her, 'but as his work did not interest me I never sought to know him'. She unpacked her fine lay figure, acquired a tall oak easel, paints, brushes and Jacobean furniture, then wrote to Brooks without giving her address to tell him she needed solitude to work.

Brooks scoured London until he found her. From the safe side of the front door Romaine told him she would go to the end of the earth to avoid him and that if he did not go away and leave her alone, she would stop his allowance. He went back to Capri. She allowed him £300 a year and resisted his appeals for more.

Brooks spent the rest of his life on Capri. He worked at his sonnets in which every word was to be perfect, and he developed a bizarre piano technique of crossing over the fingers of the same hand to play descending notes. When the sonnets were rejected by publishers he began a translation of Greek epigrams.

For a time he lived with the novelist E.F. Benson, in a white-washed hillside house with a steep garden and a big studio. Benson said of Brooks that he made less of fine abilities and educated tastes than anyone he had ever met. When Benson eventually settled in Lamb House in Rye, Brooks moved to a one-bedroomed cottage on Capri, the Villa Salvia.

He quarrelled with friends over trivial things, but depended on them for money. When they moved from the island, his world

5 John Singer Sargent (1856–1925). Born in Florence of American parents, he moved to Paris in 1884 to study with Carolus-Duran, then to England in 1886.

contracted and he was a great deal alone. His house was a climb from the town and cold in winter. Coal for the fire and cooking stove was expensive. A maid cooked his midday meal and made his bed. In the afternoons he pottered in the garden and walked his fox terriers.

The seasons drifted past. In May 1929 he became ill and went to a clinic in Naples for tests and X-rays, which revealed inoperable cancer of the liver and after three days he returned to Capri. The day before he died the post brought him a package from the publisher to whom he had sent his epigrams. A similar volume had recently appeared so his manuscript was returned. 'Somewhere,' E.F. Benson said, 'beneath the ash of his indolence there burned the authentic fire.'

For a time Romaine felt banished from Capri because of Brooks. In London in 1903 she immersed herself in the work of serious painters and resolved to find her own style. She bought several watercolours on silk by Charles Conder,[6] 'gossamer-like lines with a dreamer's dim memory of colour', and a painting of the Doge's palace by Walter Sickert.[7] She was drawn to art nouveau and the Decadents – Max Beerbohm, Aubrey Beardsley, Oscar Wilde. She admired Whistler most – for 'the subtlety of his tones', and thought his technique perfect but that he lacked surprise. Portrait painting was to be her genre, but she wanted her own 'disturbed temperament' to express complex and indeterminate moods. She painted portraits of 'a uniform melancholy', however jaunty the headgear and shawls. One, of a young man with a bowed head and pink

---

6 Charles Conder (1868–1909), English-born impressionist painter who settled in Australia. He began painting on silk in 1891.

7 Walter Richard Sickert (1860–1942), British painter and engraver. The crime writer Patricia Cornwell claims there is forensic evidence that he was Jack the Ripper.

tie, was accepted for an exhibition. 'Even such light success as that
brought encouragement.'

Like Natalie and Olive Custance, Romaine found Bosie attrac-
tive; she saw him as a *lapidé*, like herself. She met him at the house
of Robbie Ross,[8] who had been the first of Wilde's lovers, and was
surprised by his 'blond, boyish youthfulness'. In 1904 he gave her
a book of his poems *The City of the Soul* and inscribed it with:
'We have often said imperishable things.'

That autumn Romaine went to Cornwall and rented a studio
in St Ives, 'the very place where one could study an ever-changing
opalescent sea'. At high tide the sea dashed against the walls. She
worked to reproduce 'an endless gamut of greys', wanting to paint
nuances she could scarcely perceive. She felt she had been over-
influenced by the brightness of southern Italy and that her use of
colour lacked range and subtlety.

She studied in the company of artists who formed the caucus
of what became known as the Newlyn Group, painting pastoral
scenes of Cornish life: Lamorna Birch,[9] Walter Langley,[10] Ralph
Todd.[11] She attended a school of painting, started in 1899 by Elizabeth and Stanhope Forbes,[12] for 'the student who wishes seriously

---

8   Robert Baldwin 'Robbie' Ross (1869–1918), art dealer and writer, Wilde's lover (when
    he was seventeen and Wilde thirty-one) and his literary executor. His ashes were placed
    in Wilde's grave when he died.

9   Samuel John Lamorna Birch (1869–1955) named himself after the Lamorna Valley,
    where he settled.

10 Walter Langley (1852–1922) went to Newlyn two years before Stanhope Forbes. He
    later moved to Penzance.

11 Ralph Todd (1852–1932) worked mainly in watercolour. He went to Newlyn in 1884,
    then moved to Helston.

12 Stanhope Forbes (1857–1947) went to Newlyn in 1884 and painted *Fish Sale on a
    Cornish Beach* the following year. He stayed in Newlyn until he died. He married Eliz-
    abeth Armstrong in 1889. She liked painting children – *School is Out* and *Jean, Jeanne,
    Jeannette*.

to study painting and drawing according to the recent developments in English art'.

Each Saturday there was criticism of work in progress. At other students' studios Romaine saw paintings of Newlyn harbour, boats and fishermen, picnics and beach parties at St Ives, the fair at Penzance. She was asked for a reciprocal visit:

I was at first most reluctant. Why I finally changed my mind is hard to imagine. I lined up on my mantelpiece a dozen or so of the small pieces of cardboard each showing a successful or unsuccessful grey attempt. There were no boats, no fishermen. My guests finding nothing to look at trooped out of my studio in silence. I had been judged half-witted by them and I knew it; but as usual I preferred just such deprecation where there could be no converging of views.

She held her individuality in high regard and would not identify with any group, or become attached to any place.

When she returned to London she intended to paint portraits in the tones of the wintry English ocean, but though her chosen colour was grey, London fog depressed her. She felt she had internalised the ghosts of her mother and brother, 'they are now one with us'. She disliked her cook and maid, and was disturbed by hymn-singing in a nearby chapel and by the sight of sick children at a hospital across the street.

She was lonely and missed Capri, but felt she could not return because of Brooks. Wanting her mood to lift, she wrote to her gardener there and asked him to send his son to work for her. Giovanni arrived. To evoke the brightness, warmth and light of

Capri, Romaine dressed him in a blue blouse, trousers with a red sash and a knotted scarf. He hated it, complained that he was ridiculed by men in the street and asked to dress as an English butler. Romaine found him a job as a waiter in an Italian restaurant but soon heard that he had gone to Buenos Aires to become a market gardener. She moved again to Paris.

15

Sitting high on a stool at the Ace Bar, waiting for my blind date, my Soulmate, from the 'Women Seeking Women' section of the Sunday paper. Drinking Glenfiddich with a splash of water. Big-bottomed girls with shorn hair take their beer in pints. No plumed hats, jewels, or designer frocks here.

Alice B. Toklas said Natalie acquired her more casual lovers in the toilets of a department store. My date is apparently a poet. By e-mail she has told me of her thirty-year-old daughter, and how a year ago her own lover, Desirée, died in her arms. She is interested in palaeontology, the arts, and fly-fishing and would like to meet someone with a sense of humour. Perhaps she will book into a hotel with me tonight. Unless some minor impediment surfaces to such a brazen declaration of need.

19

Paris

'Sometimes we get what we want and it is not what we wanted.'

In Paris in 1905 Romaine bought a house in the Avenue du Trocadéro in the sixteenth arrondissement. She decorated it as solipsistically as had her mother the Château Grimaldi but in opposing style. She used muted effects and scarce colour to reflect her sense of self. At roof level she had a glass studio with views of the Seine and the Eiffel Tower. She wanted each room, and all the furniture and pictures, to be in spatial harmony and to provide backgrounds for her paintings. Every aspect of the interior was contrived by her, with hanging brocades, screens, glass, old wood furniture, and black-bordered pale grey velvet carpet.

She had an English chauffeur, a French maid, a Spanish concierge, and a Belgian chef, and she dressed in ermine, velvet and pearls. 'Her gowns like her home all have the individual touch,' an American journalist wrote. A self-portrait done that year showed her veiled in black – it was a point of pride to portray herself as elegantly martyred. Commissions for portraits came from society women, and she made much of their haute couture and inner loss.

Hers was the culture of Paris's Right Bank, of baronesses, marquesses, princesses and the stylish rich.

Most of her portraits were of women: *Woman in a Black Hat*, *Woman in a Green Hat*, *The Flowered Hat*. The hats were ornate, the clothes concealing, the faces passive and unsmiling. White became the source of light in her painting – azaleas, carnations, a china bowl. Balconies figured and distant ships. In one of her best early portraits, *The White Bird*, a young woman in white, buttoned to the neck, stands by a screen and a caged bird. The only colour is from the bird's beak and the feather in the woman's hat.

Romaine was uninterested in conversing in French or Italian, had a poor memory for names and facts, and never answered letters that praised her work. She knew of Natalie Barney, her liking for experiment in art, her house in Neuilly where lesbians danced in the garden, but she held aloof from such gaiety. She said she had no need for people and did not want a social life. None the less aspects of her and Natalie's Paris life elided. Lady Anglesey, 'Minnie', was a mutual friend. Romaine described her as pale and delicate, like a porcelain figure. 'She was distinctive and elegant, her thoughts feathery and confident, her concentration non-existent. She chirped and twittered.' Romaine wanted to paint her, but Minnie would only agree if Romaine made her look thirty. The portrait never happened.

In 1907 Romaine, too, had an affair with Renée Vivien. 'I found myself drifting along with her. She had never freed herself from an early sorrow and she sought relief.' Romaine thought her affected and childish and spoke of the claptrap of her surroundings: the incense and the Louis XVI men's clothes, the phosphorescent Buddhas and the tunnel-shaped bed lit from within. But she was drawn to her melancholy and poetic gift: 'If ghosts were wont to visit and haunt me, she, pale life, visited and haunted death.'

Renée told her that La Brioche, the Baronne van Zuylen, was jealous. 'I willingly believed her and made it the pretext to end our friendship. But she had taken this indirect way hoping to attach me still further. Someone came to intercede for her ... I would not go back ... a few months afterwards I heard she was dead.'

Such liaisons, Romaine was warned, would tarnish her reputation as a *femme du monde*. She said she did not care and hoped to 'give them something to talk about, something to shock them thoroughly, one way or the other – "they" being the idle and stupid tribe called society'. She described her burgeoning success as an artist as a form of capitulation, which trapped her when it ought to have been an escape. She called the artistic world a hothouse: 'L'esprit was the highest achievement and "les bons mots" rattled up against the low glass roof, but never did a sharp vigorous thought break through to let in the fresh air.'

After Renée Vivien, Romaine had an affair with the Princesse de Polignac[1] who was described by Proust as icy as a cold draught and with Dante's profile. The princess, ten years older than Romaine, had a liking for relationships with a sado-masochistic undertow. Born Winnaretta Singer, she was the eighteenth child of Isaac Singer, inventor of the sewing machine. She talked through her

---

1 Winnaretta Singer (1865–1943). Among her other lesbian lovers were her husband's niece, Armande de Polignac, Olga de Meyer, thought to be the Prince of Wales's daughter – and Violet Trefusis. Some of Proust's evocations of salon culture came from attending her gatherings. She used her fortune to benefit the arts and commissioned new musical works to be performed at her salon: Stravinsky's *Renard*, Satie's *Socrate*, and Poulenc's *Concerto for Two Pianos*.

teeth, wore high necked gowns, and spoke French with no concession to accent.

Her mansion at the corner of the Avenue Henri-Martin and the rue Cortambet was reconstructed in eighteenth-century French classical style and fitted with galleries and concert rooms. She filled it with Renaissance tapestries and paintings by Goya, Manet, Monet, Renoir and Degas.[2] In her *grand salon* she held concerts and exhibitions of paintings, including her own.

Her first marriage, to Prince Louis de Scey-Montbéliard, was arranged by her mother.[3] Winnaretta declined sex with him, accused him of cruelty and paid the Vatican for an annulment. Her second was to Prince Edmond de Polignac[4] in 1893 when she was twenty-eight and he was nearly sixty. He was homosexual and an impecunious composer of derivative choral music and melodies. Edmond de Goncourt[5] in his journal said the marriage was agreed 'on condition that the husband does not enter his wife's bedroom and on the payment of a sum of money which might permit him to mount his music which the opera houses do not want'.

---

2 All were Modernists in art who broke from conventions of representation. The impressionists showed reality in transient effects of light and colour. Francisco de Goya (1746–1828): 'the first of the moderns'. Spanish court painter. His etchings 'The disasters of War', not published until after his death, depict the horrors of the Napoleonic invasion of Spain. Édouard Manet (1832–83), his *Le Déjeuner sur l'herbe*, when first shown at the Salon des Refusés in 1863, was attacked by reviewers. Claude Monet (1840–1926): for 43 years he lived at Giverny. He painted the lake and gardens he created there. August Renoir (1841–1917): French impressionist who painted the middle class at leisure. Edgar Degas (1834–1917): French impressionist. 'Only when the artist no longer knows what he is doing, does he do good things,' he said.

3 American money was often traded for European titles. Winnaretta was twenty-two when she was married off to Prince Scey-Montbéliard.

4 Prince Edmond de Polignac (1834–1901). He died after eight years of marriage.

5 Edmond de Goncourt (1822–96), French writer, critic and publisher. He bequeathed his entire estate to found and fund the most prestigious French literary prize, the annual Prix Goncourt. Marcel Proust won it. And Simone de Beauvoir.

At the Paris salons and the Palazzo Polignac, a fifteenth-century Lombardesque palace in Venice, Romaine socialised with Jean Cocteau, Colette, Paul Valéry, Poulenc, Proust, Diaghilev, Nijinsky, Pavlova, and Ida Rubinstein.[6] She credited the princess with her own mother's stubborn strength and said her arched nose and protruding lower lip showed 'atavistic ruthlessness'. The princess commissioned her portrait. Robert de Montesquiou said Romaine made her look like the murderous Roman emperor Nero, only a thousand times more cruel.

In 1910 Romaine had her first solo exhibition, which opened on 2 May at the Galéries Durand-Ruel.[7] She covered the red walls with beige and showed thirteen of her portraits but not the one of Winnaretta. Included were Madame Eugenia Errázuris, with a false smile under a mound of quivering ostrich feathers, the Princess Lucien Murat, dressed to kill and, in contrast, anonymous nudes of skinny girls.

Reviews were good. Claude Roger-Marx[8] wrote of Romaine's cold irony and perspicacity: 'the soul is identified with the flesh'. Arsène Alexandre[9] commended her originality. De Montesquiou, in *Le Figaro*, called her the 'Thief of Souls' and said that the most brilliant of Paris society fêted her. He praised her candour, ingenuity,

---

6 The Ballets Russes thrilled European audiences from 1909–14. The first season was a major event in the artistic life of Paris. Serge Diaghilev (1872–1929) was director of the Ballets Russes. Vaslav Nijinsky (1888–1950), Anna Pavlova (1881–1931) and Ida Rubinstein (1885–1960) were principal dancers.

7 Renoir in 1882 painted the brothers Charles and Georges Durand-Ruel, and Paul Durand-Ruel's daughters. The family had galleries in Paris and London, gave exhibitions to Monet, Pissarro, Mary Cassatt, Renoir, and bought their work.

8 Claude Roger-Marx (1888–1977), author of books on Rembrandt, Bonnard, Toulouse-Lautrec and Utrillo.

9 Arsène Alexandre (1859–1937), art critic and author of books on Bakst, modern art, French posters and book covers.

and her juxtaposition of the comic and tragic. Commissions followed. Jean Cocteau posed on her balcony, with a view of the Eiffel Tower as a symbol of modernism (he had written a poem about it), Gabriele d'Annunzio and Ida Rubinstein commissioned portraits from her.

Romaine became a notable Paris lesbian, living for art, in the city where modernism flourished, the climate was accepting and the spirit free. Dismissive of success, she said it inspired malice, and that exposing her inner self to the world made her feel vulnerable and like a prisoner: angry, impatient, and marking time. Rather than paint, she preferred to read and study alone in her library, and she talked of returning to her simple life on Capri. Beneath all she did was her expressed desire to be elsewhere, to exist in a vacuum, without attention from anyone.

20

Gabriele D'Annunzio

'Literature is becoming quite unliveable.'

In her *Blue Notebooks* Liane de Pougy wrote of meeting Gabriele D'Annunzio at a lunch party in Florence in 1902. He gave her an inscribed copy of his play *Francesca da Rimini*, wrapped in parchment and tied with green ribbon. He also invited her to visit his Villa Capponcina and sent a rose-filled carriage to collect her.

He had written the play the previous year for the 'divine Eleonora Duse',[1] the most illustrious of his numberless lovers. Inspired by their own destructive relationship, and the Fifth Canto of Dante's *Inferno*, it was a tragedy, in verse, set in the thirteenth century, of guilty love, passion and brutality. Duse starred in it, rehearsed the large cast, supervised the sets and financed the entire production.

D'Annunzio's Villa Capponcina, set in vineyards and olive groves, was high on a hill overlooking Florence. He had filled it with Grecian statues, antique armour, illuminated missals and old harps

---

1 Eleonora Duse (1858–1924), Italian actress, revered for her interpretations of Ibsen's heroines and as *La Dame aux Camélias*.

As Liane stepped from her carriage a line of servants threw hand-fuls of roses at her. D'Annunzio's conversation was, she said, 'marvel-lous':

> But there before me was a frightful gnome with red-rimmed eyes and no eyelashes, no hair, greenish teeth, bad breath, the manners of a mountebank and the reputation, nevertheless, for being a ladies' man, and a man who was, to say the least, ungrateful to the ladies. I used every trick to resist him and escaped by promising to return. Two days later he sent the same carriage for me. I substituted my maid for myself, my sniffy old Adèle with a note, a long note . . .

Romaine met D'Annunzio in 1909 at a lunch given by Robert de Montesquiou. He was forty-six, she was thirty-five. She was intrigued by his pale face, the way he used his knife and fork 'like weapons', his Nietzschean view of himself as superman, his erudition and perversity. She sensed, she said, a 'supernatural force', a cruel energy: 'To me, he represented the great *lapidé* of our times.' She thought his writing 'elemental'. All his novels, plays, and poems were proscribed by the Vatican.

They went riding in the Bois: he gave her books, a dog she named Puppy, and a photograph of himself when young, dressed in white and flanked by wolfhounds at the edge of a dark forest. He liked her apartment, said she was a true artist and called her 'Cinerana', 'little ashen one', for the grey tones she used in her paintings.

Romaine said he lifted her from despondency, but 'past trials had wrought for me an armour of the hardest metal so, though very much attracted by his personality, I remained immune. His fire could warm me but it could not burn.' Such immunity suited D'Annunzio who fantasised about sex with lesbians and courted rejection. Natalie said of him that whereas she only liked men from ear to forehead he only liked women from the waist down. He told Romaine how debts and bankruptcy had forced him to flee Italy, and of how his *amica tormentosa*, Donatella, the Countess de Goloubeff,[2] had pursued him to Paris and was daily sending him threatening letters.

Out of a desire to help him, in the summer of 1910 Romaine rented the Villa St Dominique at Moulleau, near Arcachon. Her hope was for them to live together in creative calm. She would paint his portrait, he was to write *The Martyrdom of Saint Sebastian*, which was to be a showpiece for his writing and for Ida Rubinstein's dance and mime. Romaine's chauffeur, Mr Bird from Lambeth, drove her there from Paris. She hired servants and a cook and set up work rooms for herself and D'Annunzio. To avoid Donatella, he travelled from Paris under the pseudonym of Monsieur Guy d'Arbes. Trunks of his clothes arrived later from Italy and he posed for his portrait wearing a jacket in hunting pink.

St Sebastian was to be a five-act symbolist fantasy in French verse, sexually ambiguous, with music by Debussy and sets and costumes by Bakst.[3] D'Annunzio called Ida Rubinstein a fabulous being, like Botticelli's Venus, a creature of genius with perfect legs. He had admired her as Zobeida, swept away by Nijinsky, the Sultan's Golden Slave, in Diaghilev's 1910 production of

---

2 Nathalie de Goloubeff's affair with D'Annunzio lasted, with bizarre interludes, from 1908 to 1915, during which time she continued to share a house with her husband, Count Viktor Golubev, a wealthy Russian diplomat.

3 Leon Bakst (1866–1924). Stage and costume designer for the Ballets Russes.

Schéhérazade. In her own production of Oscar Wilde's *Salome*, choreographed by Michel Fokine,[4] Ida had excited audiences by appearing nude. She took the lead roles in *Cleopatra, La Dame aux camélias,* and Stravinsky's *Ice Maiden.* She challenged the Ballets Russes with her Ballets Ida Rubinstein. Natalie admired her transsexual roles: as Orpheus and as Cupid in *Les Noces de Psyche,* and was also impressed by a photograph, that was to appear in the *Dancing Times,* of Ida in trousers and knee-length leather boots.

In the *Martyrdom* Ida was to speak as well as dance. By casting her as Sebastian, a Lebanese soldier, D'Annunzio turned her into his androgynous anti-hero. Sebastian shoots an arrow towards heaven and it fails to return to earth. Inspired by such a miracle he converts to Christianity. The Emperor Diocletian, who is in love with him, demands that before abandoning Apollo for Christ he must prove the miracle. Sebastian dances on hot coals, which turn to lilies, heals a sick woman, and when shot to death with arrows his soul flies to heaven.

Ida went to Arcachon to discuss the script. As a present, she took D'Annunzio a tortoise with a gilded shell. She practised shooting arrows into pine trees, courted his approval of her performance, and resisted his attempts at seduction. After a week she left for Monte Carlo to rehearse her dance sequences with Fokine.

Romaine was contemptuous of D'Annunzio's sexual interest in Ida. Her hopes for a creative haven ended when Mr Bird announced that a blonde woman with a revolver was climbing over the garden gates. It was Donatella, intent on killing Romaine, her 'mortal enemy'. Deterred, she moved into a neighbouring villa and became

---

4 Michel Fokine (1880–1942), choreographer, who joined Diaghilev's Ballets Russes in 1909.

dramatically ill. D'Annunzio went into depression. Romaine accused him of contriving such scenes, left for Paris, then wrote saying she pitied Donatella. 'Once she moved near to us I was troubled and felt myself very much to blame.'

D'Annunzio pleaded for Romaine to return to Arcachon. She made extravagant excuses: she had crushed her hand in a door, she suffered from blood clots and chronic bronchitis. She was, she said, disappointed in the way he had misunderstood her efforts to protect him. 'I felt you were unfortunate like all true geniuses. You brought your troubles to me and I opened my arms to you and wanted to shield you with my love.' But he had belittled her. 'Dear friend believe me,' she wrote:

> true love does not simply consist of the banal and brutal act. There
> are so many other things whose very existence you ignore . . . Your
> destructive power is stronger than you and everything that comes
> near you is annihilated . . . I had hoped, because I had so much
> respect for your art you would have had a little for mine. But it
> was not so. I was for you only another *female* to destroy.

He had, she said, endeavoured to reduce her to the level of a street tart. She signed herself 'Fratello', his brother, told him she was a great artist with a divine talent, that her emotions were pure while his were vulgar, and that though she had hoped to find in him 'a throne higher than my own', once again she had paid the price for being mistaken. As for his declaration of madness:

> I cannot understand it. You have all you want from life. I foresee
> to the day you die an endless number of legs to explore – what

boundless joy! Even in heaven, dear poet, there will be reserved for you an enormous octopus with an infinite number of women's legs and no head. Forgive my candour.

He replied in hyperbole, alluding to the diamond of her heart that his fire could not melt. 'Standing between bleak sky and foaming waters, you fear not the shock of the tenth wave.'[5]

In time they restored a sort of respect and kept a cautious friendship, though Romaine would not suffer any assault on her dignity: she had the authority of money, a belief that she was a genius, and an impressive will. But to appease D'Annunzio's creditors, when an auction of his possessions was held at the Villa Capponcina, she paid for him to keep his library and a portrait of his mother by Basilio Cascella.[6]

The next summer she completed his portrait. He stayed at a villa she hired at St Jean de Luz, and each morning posed on the terrace for her 'like a soldier': behind him were waves crashing over a breakwater.

The curator of the Luxembourg Museum bought the picture when he saw it at her Paris studio. D'Annunzio said of it that he could accept the mouth but not the eyes. As a reparative move, in an article about her, published in *Illustrazione* in April 1913, he wrote with all grace of her 'guarded sensitivity', her insight into character, her free spirit and her subtle orchestration of greys. She kept the manuscript copy of this article locked in a carved box.

---

5 Every tenth wave is said to be the biggest. Ivan Aivazovsky painted *The Tenth Wave* in 1850.

6 Basilio Cascella (1860–1950), Italian painter, lithographer, sculptor, tailor, and photographer. His two sons were also artists. There is a Cascella Museum in Pescara.

16

I met Martha and her husband in the park for a picnic. We lay under a cherry tree with a view of the pond and birds. There were buttercups in the grass. My friends had not been lovers for many years but in this sparkling setting seemed cautiously fond. Michael joked of a fantasy of joining Martha and me in bed. I said, but Martha isn't a lesbian. Martha stared at the herbaceous border. There was a brief silence. I feared the spoiling of the day and was glad of the diversion of a heron in a willow tree with a carp in its beak.

21

Ida Rubinstein

'Which of all our pasts will be the Past?'

Le Martyre de St Sébastien opened in Paris on 22 May 1911 at the Théâtre du Châtelet.[1] Ida mimed, danced and recited through dazzling scene changes, with an orchestra of a hundred musicians, and a chorus of two hundred voices. It all lasted five hours, until one in the morning, though many in the audience slipped away before the end. There were nine performances.

Response to it was mixed. Reviewers called it decadent, flamboyant, incoherent; they had difficulty with D'Annunzio's French verse and Ida's thick Russian accent. Jean Cocteau compared her to a stained-glass figure, miraculously animated. Proust thought her legs sublime. Lily de Gramont called it 'a symphony that makes you believe in heaven because it takes you there'. Natalie found D'Annunzio's prose pompous and high-blown. De Montesquiou went to every performance and spoke of Ida's charisma and allure. The Vatican

---

1 The Théâtre du Châtelet opened in 1862. Seating 2,500, it had remarkable acoustics and a steep rake. It staged concerts, operas, ballets and, later, films. Debussy, Strauss and Mahler conducted their own music there.

added the play to its Index of obscene works, offensive to Christians.

After the first night Romaine went backstage to congratulate Ida who was exhausted. 'She was seated, curved over, as if the wings of martyrdom had carried away their triumph.' To take revenge on D'Annunzio for the pain he had caused her, Romaine then began an affair with Ida.

Romaine described her as like an apparition, a mystery:

> I remember one cold snowy morning walking with Ida around the Longchamps racecourse. Everything was white and she wore a long ermine coat and under it a white feathery garment. Her coat was open and exposed her frail bare chest and slender neck. Her face sharply cut with long golden eyes and a delicate bird-like nose; her partly veiled head with dark hair moving gracefully from the temples as though the wind were smoothing it back.

Ida came from a rich Russian Jewish family and had been orphaned as a child. She had married to free herself from her repressive guardians and to pursue a dancing career. Like Romaine she soon left her husband and like her enjoyed a large inherited income. For Ida, art, performance and life were indivisible. She kept monkeys and a black panther as pets, employed retinues of servants, and lived in suites of rooms in grand hotels. She owned a private yacht, the *Istar*, and wore gold-lamé pyjamas, boleros covered in jewels, and plumed turbans fastened with diamond brooches.

After the First World War she travelled widely, camping in Sardinia, hunting elks in Norway and lions in Africa. She took with her a large staff, and tents equipped as bathrooms, kitchens, and reception rooms. 'I am now on the shores of the lake at Bangwuolo, which I believe is the most beautiful place in the world,' she wrote to de Montesquiou in September 1921. Or, 'I am writing to you here, right at the source of the Blue Nile, in a mysterious forest full of orchids and violets, leopards and apes.'

In her studio with its long glass terrace with white flowers and black and crystal décor, Romaine took photographs of Ida lying nude on a divan. To satirise D'Annunzio's St Sebastian fantasy, she painted a picture of her naked and bound to a post, looking bored, while a dwarfish masked archer in a skirt shoots an arrow at her. She then invited D'Annunzio to her studio for a private viewing.

Ida became her muse. In *The Crossing* (c.1911), which Romaine variously called *The Passing*, *Death*, or *Femme Morte*, she painted her lying on a white wing, flying through darkness, dead, or asleep. In *The Weeping Venus*, too, she was dead or sleeping, incorporeal and deathly white. In an oil sketch of 1912, she was half naked and about to wing off into the ether. Romaine seemed influenced equally by Aubrey Beardsley's art-nouveau, D'Annunzio's lurid symbolism, and her mother's astral planes.

Ida described Romaine as beautiful 'like an orchid'. She wanted to live with her and for them to buy a farmhouse in the French countryside. In the summer of 1914 they were travelling in Switzerland when Germany declared war on France. They took a train back to Paris. Romaine turned her cellar into a bomb shelter and stored her paintings in Bordeaux. She set up a fund for wounded French artists; Ida funded a hospital run from the Carlton hotel.

In a picture called the *The Cross of France*, Romaine painted Ida cloaked in black, her head swathed in white, the insignia of the red cross on her shoulder, the town of Ypres burning in the background. D'Annunzio wrote an accompanying poem linking Christ's suffering to a nation at war. The poem and painting were bound in a brochure and sold to raise money for the Red Cross.[2]

For D'Annunzio, war offered an ecstatic pursuit of battle, a fascistic expression of the superiority of the Italian race, and an opportunity to live out his fantasy of himself as superman. He returned to Italy, became the commander of an aerial unit based near Venice and wrote jingoistic articles for *La Corriere della sera* exhorting Italians to violence and self-sacrifice, and calling for the restoration of Italy to classical greatness: 'If it is considered a crime to incite the citizenry to violence I glory in that crime . . . Every excess of force is allowable if it serves to prevent the loss of our Fatherland.'

In 1916 Romaine rented a villa on the Zattere in Venice, so as to paint him again, this time as *Il Commandante*, in military cloak and tunic, intent on victory and conquest, his right fist clasping some phallic rod. To the emergent fascists, he was a military hero.

After the war D'Annunzio was elected president of the Italian Academy by Mussolini. He bought a seventeenth-century farmhouse by Lake Garda, called it the Vittoriale and filled it with art and curiosities: statues of Greek slaves and horses, Chinese pots and Buddhas, a headless statue lying horizontal on a divan. The dining room glowed in gold, the Blue Bathroom had 2000 knick-knacks in it – plaques, ceramic animals, plates. In the Room of the Relics was an altar, covered with Baroque religious paraphernalia, and at its centre the crushed steering wheel of the motorboat in which Sir Henry Segrave died while breaking the water-speed record on Lake Windermere in 1930.[3] Opposite it was a wall tapestry of a priest holding up his hand with

---

2 In 1920 Romaine was awarded the Legion d'Honneur for the service to France of her art.

3 Henry Segrave (1896–1930) made three runs on 11 June 1930 in his boat *Miss England II*. On the second he travelled at a record 101 mph. On the third, his boat hit debris, flew into the air, then crashed into the water. He died two hours later.

the woven motto: 'Five are the fingers, five are the sins.'

As D'Annunzio aged, he used prostitutes and cocaine for sexual thrills, though his fascination with lesbians abided.[4] Romaine said his vitality inspired her and elevated her from the mundanity of being a portrait painter of fashionable women. But her best work was of closed and inward-looking figures in domestic interiors. The superwoman stance she conferred on Ida Rubinstein, and the staring eyes of genius she gave D'Annunzio in her portraits of him, had the coercive feel of propaganda art and were a reminder of St Mar's disturbing gaze.

In the triangle Romaine formed with D'Annunzio and Ida Rubinstein, Narcissus ruled. After the war Ida bought a large house in Paris at 7 Place des états Unis. Bakst designed the interior: a studio with blue friezes, a grand drawing room with Abyssinian wall-hangings and Japanese furniture, and a garden where flowers in trays – mauve hyacinths, red azaleas, white lilies – were changed to match her dress of the day.

Romaine tired of such self-absorption. During the First World War, at a tea party of what she called 'American society women of the "pouter pigeon" variety', she heard one of them say to Lady Anglesey, 'Natalie Barney will be received again in society when she returns to her mother's friends.' Romaine was curious: 'Looking round at these smug and puffed out members of Society, I decided that Natalie Barney had doubtless made more inspiring friends elsewhere.' At Romaine's request, Lady Anglesey arranged for the two women to meet. 'Natalie was a miracle,' Romaine said. 'As fresh as a spring morning. I had never found a real woman friend before.'

---

4 In 1926 Tamara de Lempicka painted lesbian nudes, had a cocaine-hyped dalliance with D'Annunzio and was the lover of the Duchesse de la Salle.

NATALIE AND ROMAINE

22

Natalie and Romaine

'Nothing can separate me from my Angel.
Ever and for ever Nat Nat.'

They schmoozed together and called it 'dancey prancey'. Romaine was Angel, or Angel Birdie, Natalie was Nat Nat. They were 'Darling' to each other. When they met, in 1915, Romaine was forty-one, Natalie thirty-nine. Together they read Freud and Jung, James Joyce and D.H. Lawrence, 'but not his novels'.

Natalie was drawn to Romaine's strangeness and vulnerability. She said Romaine had no disguise, no pose and was 'a real head and soul in an unreal world'. She tirelessly told her she was beautiful and a genius, her singing voice perfect, her paintings immortal. Romaine was, she said, dearer to her than her own life. 'I love my Angel better than anything else in the world and prove it.' In return, she asked only that Romaine should need her above all others.

For Romaine, Natalie's warmth and kindness were an unfamiliar gift. Natalie was not judgemental, nor did she recoil from the drama of Romaine's life, but the relationship was based on an understanding that Romaine must be above comparison. Romaine said that Natalie 'had an unusual mind of the best quality', but she decried her Friday salons as gatherings of drunkards and society women; it was not a fair description of Gertrude Stein, Colette, Sylvia Beach, Lily de Gramont et al.

Romaine declined when Natalie's mother suggested a joint exhibition of their paintings in Washington and deplored any comparison to Alice Barney's work. In 1920 she did a portrait of Natalie with nothing wild or Amazonian about it apart from a small model of a prancing horse in tribute to de Gourmont's view. She made her look comfortable and friendly.

Their lives entwined. In Paris they lazed on the grass by the lilac bushes in the Bois de Boulogne. On Capri they stayed in the Villa Cercola, which Romaine acquired in 1918; it had terraced gardens, guest apartments and furniture made by local craftsmen. At Honfleur they stayed with Lily de Gramont. At Aix en Provence they left their hotel because of a 'bouncing' woman and her dog in rooms above theirs. They opened a joint Swiss bank account (Natalie's sister Laura managed their finances). Natalie talked of their being together for the rest of their lives and of sharing the same grave: 'My angel is my only real companion and friend.'

But from the start, practical problems were hard to overcome. Paris, and her Friday salons at 20 rue Jacob were essential to Natalie. If she and Romaine lived in the same house, or near to each other, as she hoped, and 'walked out hand in hand at the end of the day', it would have to be in Paris – which Romaine called a desert, 'wanting in all calm, beauty and dignity'. 'No Paris for me,' she wrote. 'I suppose an artist must live alone and feel free otherwise all individuality goes. I can think of my painting only when I am alone, even less do any actual work.'

She shared her mother's dissatisfaction with place and her indifference to society. In 1918 she took an apartment in rue Raynouard[1] with another lofty studio designed entirely to her taste, but she could not settle there. She moved on to Capri, London, New York, Florence, Venice, Nice. Wherever she went she established a seemingly perfect environment for work, then left. Natalie said she excelled in making the residences she acquired fit her laws of beauty.

After spending time with Natalie, then time apart, Romaine at first missed her greatly then 'regained that state of mind which constitutes my personal life'. She felt she lost her sense of self when they were together and was relieved to return to solitude.

Natalie understood Romaine's need to keep her identity intact and knew how brittle that identity was. But in their separations she feared Romaine would not find reunion essential. She struggled with doubt and despair at Romaine's equivocation and the 'relentless quality' that made Natalie behave towards her like some 'dumb, devoted, pitiable animal'.

Natalie's devotion overruled her doubts. In Washington in summer 1920, while Romaine was on Capri, Natalie read through a trunk of letters: 'Letters from Eva and from Renée, both dead to me, the one through life, the other through and even before death. Yet you, I sometimes feel, are steadfast even through change, and fond of your Natalie enduringly, as I am of my angel.'

Steadfastness had its tests. Romaine found Natalie's enthusiasms and multiple love affairs **hard** to endure. In summer 1922 she

---

1 Rue Raynouard, in the sixteenth arrondissement. Lily de Gramont lived at no. 67, Natalie's sister Laura was at 74; Balzac had lived at no. 47.

agreed to meet her and Lily de Gramont in Calvados for a holiday. Natalie wrote an excited letter about proposed arrangements: Was the Renault in mechanical order, had Romaine got all her papers, would she find out about maps and roads, could they fit their trunks and Romaine's maid into Natalie's Buick, various friends would meet up with them at Chambourcy, they could all go to Capri.

Romaine's reply was brutal: Natalie's letter was dreadful and the complications of her life terrible. She had no intention of carrying out any of her instructions, nor did she want to see any of Natalie's friends on Capri. Natalie should count her out; she intended to holiday alone on the Italian coast. Natalie, she said, had many friends and she, Romaine, but one 'and therein lies the difference. Always remember, Nat, that I prefer Nat Nat to being alone, but alone to being with anyone else.'

Natalie, as ever, tried to be reparative and to free Romaine from any sense of obligation. But Romaine's haughtiness and selfishness grated on Lily de Gramont: 'Mrs Brooks,' she wrote in her memoir, 'puts bars on the windows of her various establishments to keep out the disappointing human race, and now no longer knows who is the prisoner.'

Nor did Romaine keep to her preference for being either with Natalie or alone. She provoked jealousy as well as suffering it. After the war she again painted on Capri. In letters she hinted to Natalie of amorous involvement with the pianist Renata Borgatti, famed for her Debussy recitals. She painted her playing at a grand piano, her short hair sleeked behind her ears, her jaw strong, hands huge, her clothes severe. 'So Renata Borgatti is "on to you" as we say,' Natalie wrote. 'I am alone and you are with her.'

I know you have not bathed without everyone on that island desiring you – that they would follow the glimmer of your perfect form to the ends of the earth – yet can any of them but me so grasp the inner goddess, the real sense of your greatness.

Also on Capri and interested in Romaine was the Marchesa Luisa Casati,[2] who bought diamond collars for her pet cheetahs, dyed her hair orange, and enhanced her green eyes with kohl and false lashes. She gave extravagant parties during the 1920s, and accrued debts of $25 million. She was painted by Boldini[3] and Augustus John,[4] sculpted by Epstein[5] and photographed by Man Ray,[6] Cecil Beaton[7] and Adolf de Meyer.[8] In her private art gallery she exhibited 130 images of herself. She too had adventures with women and the obligatory dalliance with D'Annunzio. Among her homes were the Palazzo dei Leoni[9] in Venice on the Grand Canal, and the Palais Rose, built of red marble, in Paris. Romaine wrote to Natalie that the Casati house on Capri was 'simply beautiful'. She

2 Luisa Casati (1881–1957), dubbed the patron saint of exhibitionists. In 1932 her possessions were confiscated and auctioned off to appease her creditors. She died in London and is buried with her stuffed pet Pekinese dog in Brompton Cemetery.

3 Giovanni Boldini (1845–1931), Italian-French portrait painter, commissioned by Parisian high society.

4 Augustus John (1878–1961), Welsh painter, well known for his portraits of the famous – George Bernard Shaw, Thomas Hardy, Tallulah Bankhead. He wrote two volumes of autobiography, *Chiaroscuro* and *Finishing Touches*.

5 Jacob Epstein (1880–1959), American-born sculptor who became a British citizen in 1907.

6 Man Ray (1890–1976), born Emanuel Rabinovitch in Philadelphia. A Dadaist and Surrealist photographer and painter, he moved to Paris in 1921.

7 Cecil Beaton (1904–80), English society photographer and diarist.

8 Adolf de Meyer (1868–1949), American fashion and society photographer, married to Olga de Meyer, lover to the Princesse de Polignac from 1909 to 1914. Both husband and wife were opium addicts.

9 The marchesa owned it from 1910 to 1924. Peggy Guggenheim bought it in 1948, and it houses her Venice art collection.

painted a nude portrait of the marchesa in which she made her look like some predatory bird, but was dissatisfied with it. 'It was not me,' Romaine wrote.

In their work in the 1920s, both Natalie and Romaine expressed their lesbian view. In 1921 Natalie published *Pensées d'une Amazone*. Derived from an unfinished novel, it was another collection of aphorisms and scatterings, of her tangential thoughts on life: the folly of war, the nonsense of religious dogma, and her preoccupation with love between women:

'Above all things to love.'

'We do not touch life except with our hearts.'

'You, the unfortunate happiness of my life.'

And Romaine, influenced by Natalie's quest for Sappho, became a painter of lesbians in their circle. In her studio in the rue Raynouard she painted Natalie's lovers: Lily de Gramont, untidy and with bushy eyebrows; Eyre de Lanux, bare-breasted in an icy landscape. Her portraits were bold and often life-size. She kept each of them curtained, with its own pull-cord.

Both Romaine and Natalie ignored the warnings of sexologists, and the barbs of satirists. Natalie paraded her way of loving as best:

Sick with anguish stood the crowned nine Muses about Apollo;

While the tenth sang wonderful things they knew not.

Ah, the tenth, the Lesbian!

Even while glorying this tenth muse, she and Romaine had its problems to address: how to make their own relationship enduring;

how to keep what Natalie called 'the faithful heart of us'; how to be together yet separate; how to withstand frequent 'intense and fearful partings'; how to allow each other to have other, less central, lovers and friends; and how to cope with Romaine's brittle personality which felt invaded if Natalie was in an adjacent room.

Natalie's solution was always to be conciliatory and supportive. She cared for the well-being of her 'travelling angel', and looked after her affairs and her Paris flat while Romaine was on her restless journeys. She ordered in coal to keep the place heated, sold Romaine's Renault, sent her Vichy powders for her indigestion, ointment for her haemorrhoids and thick stockings called Risque Tout from Bally. 'Don't thank Nat Nat for things I can do for you, for next to being with you, attending to you is my greatest pleasure.'

17

On the Dover train at Victoria Station heading for Brindisi then a boat to Greece – to Crete, Chios, Mykonos, Lesbos – you asked if I had any lesbian experience. I did not answer. Decades later, Mr Layzell in his breast clinic said: You have a ductal carcinoma.

Silenced by love. Silenced by death. No vocabulary for either. Do you remember the night on the ferry through the Gulf of Corinth when we lay on a coil of rope on the first-class deck. Herr Schneider came from his cabin and gave us his coat. He had seen us from his port-hole and thought we might be cold. One of those green loden coats with a swagger back that Tyrolean dentists wear. Under it we coaxed each other close. Thank you, Mr Schneider. Do you remember at Delphi when we got up at dawn to see the sun rise over the Temple of Apollo?

Looking at old photographs, at those slim dark-haired girls we once were, I remember the joy that reached to either side of those split moments, that touches again my aching heart. 'Which of all our pasts will be the past?' Natalie asked. I wonder.

23

The Monocled Lady

'To love is to see through two pairs of eyes.'

Natalie would have found it difficult to live her life as a work of art in London in the 1920s. She and Romaine might canoodle in the Avenue des Acacias but not in Regent's Park. Paris allowed such expression. In London propriety must be observed.

In 1921 a Tory member of parliament, Frederick Macquister, proposed the clause 'Acts of Gross Indecency by Females' to be added to the Criminal Law Amendment Act of 1885, which proscribed male homosexuality. In the House of Commons he pronounced that lesbianism threatened the birth rate, debauched young girls and induced neurasthenia and insanity. His clause was agreed and went to the House of Lords to be ratified.

Their lordships speculated on the effect of breaking silence on such a subject. Lord Desart[1] of Desart Court, Kilkenny, a former Director of Public Prosecutions, said: 'You are going to tell the

---

1 Sir Hamilton Cuffe, Lord Desart, was Director of Public Prosecutions when Oscar Wilde was indicted. He owned 2,063 acres of land in Ireland.

whole world there is such an offence, to bring it to the notice of women who have never heard of it, never thought of it, never dreamed of it. I think this is a very great mischief.'

Lord Birkenhead,[2] the Lord Chancellor, agreed: 'I am bold enough to say that of every thousand women, taken as a whole, 999 have never even heard a whisper of these practices. Among all these, in the homes of this country, the taint of this noxious and horrible suspicion is to be imparted.'

The legislators were afraid that 'these practices' might be contagious. Silence was to rule. Lesbians were not to cause mischief by talking of their noxious horrible lives. If they ventured out of their closeted world they did so at their peril.

Una Lady Troubridge[3] was one of the portraits in Romaine's gallery of famous lesbians. She was wife and acolyte to Radclyffe Hall, who became notorious in 1928 when her lesbian novel, *The Well of Loneliness*, was banned as obscene by the British establishment. In Paris it was thought unremarkable and a pirated edition was freely distributed. D'Annunzio wanted to send his private plane to collect a copy.

In 1923 Romaine had a studio in London at 15 Cromwell Road where Una posed with two of her fifteen dachshunds for nine sittings. Romaine depicted her as thin as a reed, her face screwed to one side to keep her monocle in place, her jacket tailored, a severe cap of hair, her shirt starched, pearls in her ears, a fob in her pocket, and a cold glint in her eye.

Throughout the sittings, Una kept up a monologue about the

2 Frederick Smith, Lord Birkenhead, Lord Chancellor (1919–22).

3 Una Elena Troubridge (1887–1963). She and Admiral Sir Ernest Troubridge divorced in 1917. Una and Radclyffe Hall (known as 'John') were partners until John's death in 1943.

Poster advertising Liane de Pougy at the Folies-Bergére, circa 1895.

Poster by Jules Cheret (1836–1932) for the Palais de Glace, where
Natalie and her lovers went ice skating.

'These drawings should be read. They evolve from the subconscious without premeditation.' Romaine Brooks, *Mummy*, 1930, also called *The Stolen Mummy* (30 x 20cm).

Romaine marked her drawings with a symbol of a wing held down by a chain. *The Idiot and the Angel*, 1930 (24 x 14cm).

The war effort: Romaine's lover, Ida Rubinstein, in 1914, the insignia of
the Red Cross on her shoulder, the town of Ypres burning behind her.
Romaine Brooks, *The Cross of France*, 1914 (oil on canvas, 115 x 191cm).

'My dead mother stands between me and life.'
Romaine Brooks, *Self-portrait*, 1923 (oil on canvas, 118 x 68cm).

'From Nat Nat's weak heart, full of love for her angel.' Romaine Brooks, *Miss Natalie Barney, 'L'Amazone'*, 1920 (oil on canvas, 86 x 65cm).

Love between Natalie and 'Lily' de Gramont evolved into a lifelong friendship. Romaine Brooks, *Elisabeth de Gramont, Duchesse de Clermont-Tonnerre*, circa 1912 (oil on canvas, 87 x 66cm).

'I was for you only another female to destroy.' Romaine Brooks, *Gabriele D'Annunzio, the Poet in Exile*, 1912, (oil on canvas, 118 x 91cm).

'So Renata Borgatti is "on to you". I am alone, and you are with her.'
Renata Borgatti (1894–1964) was well-known for her recitals of works
by Debussy and Bach. Romaine Brooks, *Renata Borgatti at the Piano*,
circa 1920 (oil on canvas, 142 x 189cm).

Truman Capote called Romaine's portraits 'the all-time ultimate gallery of famous dykes'. Romaine Brooks, *Una, Lady Troubridge*, 1924 (oil on canvas, 127 x 77cm). Una Troubridge (1887–1963) lived with Radclyffe Hall, author of the banned lesbian novel, *The Well of Loneliness*.

La Baronne Émile D'Erlanger, 1924 (oil on canvas, 106 x 86cm). The Baronne, an interior decorator, was the daughter of the Marquis de Rochegude, had houses in Paris and London, and organised the 1925 Alpine Club Gallery exhibition of Romaine's paintings.

Gluck (1895–1978), born Hannah Gluckstein into the family
that founded the Lyons & Co catering empire, was known as Peter
when young. Romaine Brooks, *Peter (A Young English Girl)* 1923–4
(oil on canvas, 92 x 62cm).

'The thief of souls.' Romaine Brooks, *Woman In A Black Hat*, 1907
(oil on canvas, 163 x 114cm).

'I had always stood alone and would proudly continue to do so.'
Romaine Brooks, *The Huntress*, 1920. Also called *Decorative Portrait of Madame de Lamaire*. (Oil on canvas, 130 x 97cm).

literary genius of 'Johnnie' (Radclyffe Hall). Both Romaine and Natalie thought Radclyffe Hall's writing trite and superficial. While Natalie wrote poems about her lady loves, and Romaine painted their portraits, novelists like Radclyffe Hall, Violet Trefusis,[4] Vita Sackville-West,[5] Colette, and Djuna Barnes concealed their lesbian relationships in *romans-à-clefs*. Johnnie was working on her second novel, *The Forge*, in which Romaine appeared as Venetia Ford, 'a strange erratic brilliant genius', a painter of monotone portraits with a dominating personality, who had studios in London, Paris and Florence and a villa on Capri, and who was beautiful 'with an elusive inward kind of beauty'.

Like Romaine, Radclyffe Hall had an awesome sense of her own importance. She said that she spoke for inverts and had the soul of a solitary. Like Romaine she too had a handsome private income and like Romaine's mother she believed herself to be in psychic communication with the dead. Romaine made overtures to her but these were resisted: 'One always feels slightly grateful of the interest shown,' said Johnnie.

Romaine had gone to London, scornful of Natalie's latest adventure with the American writer, Elizabeth Eyre de Lanux. In letters to Eyre, Natalie wrote of how she listened through the patter of the rain for her arrival, of the beautiful angle her straight shoulders made through her tailored dress, of how she would lead her to the reach of her talent and always be there for her. Romaine complained that though she herself liked going out and meeting

---

4 Violet Trefusis (1894–1972) wrote three novels, one in English and two in French about her love for Vita Sackville-West: *The Hook in the Heart* (unpublished), *Sortie de Secours* and *Broderie Anglaise*.

5 Vita Sackville-West (1892–1962). Her novel *Challenge* (first called *Rebellion*) about her love for Violet was pulped in 1920 at the instigation of her mother, Lady Sackville.

'queer dykes', a relationship for her had to have value other than the physical. She said she missed Nat Nat greatly but hoped she was getting over her 'honeymoon' while she was away.

Romaine's conundrum was irresolvable. She did not want a sustained one-to-one relationship with Natalie, with all the business of home, commitment and coupledom; she found proximity to her impossible after a short time, but she was nevertheless jealous of Natalie's pursuit of other women.

Through visitors to Natalie's salon, Romaine met London lesbians. Toupie Lowther, also known as 'Brother', during the war had managed an all-women ambulance unit in France. She lifted weights, was a tennis and fencing champion, and had crossed the alps on a motorbike with her girlfriend, Fabienne Lafargue De-Avilla, riding pillion. Toupie misconstrued what Romaine called a 'fragile *commencement*' between them, and bombarded her with phone calls and letters. Romaine told Natalie that Toupie disgusted and bored her. 'I have been very lonely. Are you coming over?'

With Radclyffe Hall and Una, Romaine lunched at the Savoy, dined at the Prince's Grill, and danced at the Cave of Harmony in Soho. At a fancy-dress party given by Teddie Gerrard,[6] who was acting in *London Calling*, a revue by Noël Coward,[7] Una was Harlequin, Radclyffe Hall an Indian chief, and Romaine a Paris workman in corduroy trousers and jacket and soft peaked cap. Among the guests were Teddie Gerrard's lover Etheline Cripps, the actresses

6 Teddie Gerrard wore backless dresses, had her black hair cut into a bob, and liked women, drink, and drugs. Gluck painted two portraits of her in 1924.

7 Noël Coward (1899–1973) was friendly with the 'lesbian *haut monde*'. Radclyffe Hall and Una Troubridge often visited him at his house Goldenhurst Farm, Aldington, near Rye.

Tallulah Bankhead and Gwen Farrar[8] who were having an affair, and the painter Gluck,[9] who chose her own monosyllabic name and dressed as a man in clothes designed by Elsa Schiaparelli.[10]

Like Romaine, Gluck was influenced by Whistler and the Newlyn school, and lived in style on inherited money. She was in her late twenties, got her shirts from Jermyn Street, had a last for her shoes at John Lobb's, the royal bootmakers, and had her hair cut at Truefitt gentlemen's hairdressers in Old Bond Street. She and Romaine agreed to paint each other.

Romaine did a large portrait of Gluck and called it *Peter, a Young English Girl*. She went to Gluck's Tite Street studio to sit for the reciprocal work. 'The elephant has come to the temple,' Gluck said of the visit. She thought Romaine's work inferior to her own and scorned her social circle as the 'lesbian *haut monde*'. She, too, wanted to paint a life-size picture, and primed a six-foot canvas. 'Romaine Brooks was a big woman,' she said in defence of its size. The encounter was not happy:

Romaine wasted so much sitting time in making a row that at last I was only left an hour in which to do what I did – but my rage and tension gave me almost superhuman powers. She

8 Tallulah Bankhead (1902–68), American screen and stage actress. She starred in *My Sin*, *Tarnished Lady*, *The Little Foxes* and *Private Lives*. She was famous for her deep raspy voice and flamboyant behaviour off-stage.

   Gwen Farrar (1899–1944), English actress and cellist.

9 Gluck (1895–1978), British painter, born Hannah Gluckstein into the family that founded the J. Lyons & Co. catering empire. Her most significant lovers were the society hostess Nesta Obermeyer, the flower expert Constance Spry, and the journalist Edith Shackleton Heald.

10 Elsa Schiaparelli (1893–1973), Italian-born avant-garde fashion designer. Her collections, like art exhibitions, were arranged around themes: the circus, or Manhattan architecture.

insisted I should do one of my 'little pictures'. I refused, so she left me with the unfinished portrait. However I had to give away many photographs of it to her friends.

Una hated Romaine's portrait of her and denied the resemblance. She told Toupie that because of it she could not again be on friendly terms with Romaine. 'Lady T is deeply displeased with me,' Romaine wrote to Natalie. The picture reflected Una's quintessential misanthropy. Romaine thought it amusing: 'It will live perhaps and cause future generations to smile.' But to avoid offending Una further, she did not include it in the London exhibition of her work at the Alpine Gallery in 1925.[11]

When Una's painting was finished, Romaine tired of London. 'All these women are so petty and uninteresting,' she wrote to Natalie. 'Send for me whenever you want me.' Natalie replied: 'When? Now? in a week, a fortnight, a month? I am ever at your command.'

Romaine motored to Dover to meet her from the boat and take her to Cromwell Road. A Monsieur Bénédite arranged a reliable *expéditeur* to have Una's portrait sent to Paris. Natalie and Romaine went to parties at Teddie Gerrard's flat in Sackville Street and at Gwen Farrar's. They planned to spend the summer in Florence and at the Villa Cercola on Capri; Una and Johnnie might meet them there. Natalie said her angel was her only real companion and friend. 'I love you very dearly and deeply. Take care, my precious angel. I most gently touch your sleeping eyelids goodnight.'

---

11 The exhibition lasted from 2 to 20 June and was arranged and financed by Baroness Emile d'Erlanger, an interior designer with a large house in Piccadilly. Romaine painted her in 1924.

18

It was not for me to out you. The governors round the boardroom table might have made your life hard. A paragraph in the Gazette *about how the Dean was seen at* Les Girls, *then slurs and innuendo about one thing or another. You needed to keep your authority, an ambitious, well-paid woman in, as ever, a man's world. So not once in our seven years together did I phone you at work, or walk arm in arm with you down your familiar streets. Your daughter's cat might signify in office natter, but I did not exist.*

24

Dolly Wilde

'People call it unnatural. All I can say is,
it's always come naturally to me.'

Dolly Wilde lived in thrall to her uncle Oscar. She was born in 1895, the year he was imprisoned, and looked like him, 'except that she was handsome', Janet Flanner said. His trials for 'gross indecency', his glittering literary career, and his humiliation by lesser men were formative influences on her. She described herself as 'more Oscar-like than he was like himself'.

Tall, with blue eyes and 'lovely, idle, opulent hands', she arrived at Natalie's salon on 28 June 1927 when she was thirty-two and Natalie was fifty. Natalie described her as 'half androgyne and half goddess. No one's presence could be as present as Dolly's.' They began a love affair that lasted fourteen years, until Dolly's death in 1941.

Once again Natalie started up a 'liaison' with a self-destructive young woman who was provoked by her infidelity, composure, and self-confidence. Within weeks Dolly wrote of feeling tortured, of 'struggling to get her hand out of the trap':

Do you love me? I wonder! Not that it matters at all. Perhaps I shan't even mind when you leave me – only then there could be no love making – *impossible* thought . . . Who will flee first? Just now I am too in love with you to dream of change . . . Did you know that it was nearly four o'clock when I left you last night? I ache with tiredness and darling I am *bruised.*

Toujours. D.

Like Natalie, Dolly wanted to charm, sparkle and live her life as a work of art, but she was chaotic. She aspired to write but could not convey in words what she really felt. She earned a little money translating from French to English works by Colette, Nancy Cunard, and Lily de Gramont, but her finances were always in a mess. She would run up bills at the Paris Ritz,[1] then leave someone else to pay. She lived in borrowed flats and rented rooms, letters sent to her went unanswered, and she did not return her library books to Sylvia Beach's Shakespeare and Company. When she went anywhere she was always late. She liked driving too fast in borrowed cars (Natalie described herself as of the era of carriages and Dolly of the era of cars). For a time she lived in Montparnasse with Marion 'Joe' Carstairs,[2] who cross-dressed, had tattoos, inherited a fortune from Standard Oil, and in her speedboat became 'the fastest woman on water'.

Janet Flanner thought Dolly was like a work of fiction, a character out of a novel: 'On the street, walking, or at a Paris

---

1 The Paris Ritz, which was designed for César Ritz by Hardouin-Mansart, the architect of Versailles, opened in 1898 on the Place Vendôme.

2 Marion 'Joe' Carstairs (1900–93), American eccentric. She had affairs with Marlene Dietrich and Tallulah Bankhead. In 1929 she bought the Caribbean island of Whale Cay where she ruled a colony of Bahamians.

restaurant table, talking. . . she seemed like someone one had become familiar with by reading, rather than by knowing.' Dolly had, she said, 'a floral quality which was the bloom of her charm'.

At parties Dolly spent too long in the lavatory and emerged with this charm enhanced. She snorted cocaine and kept a hypodermic in her bag to shoot up heroin intravenously. She then 'scintillated with epigrams' that no one could remember. In Paris she hung around restaurants and bars like Le Boeuf sur le Toit, off the Champs Élysées with the 'Jean Cocteau set'.[3] She scored her drugs from the 'marchands de paradis'. Her father, like Natalie's, had been an alcoholic.

Dolly bombarded Natalie with love letters on headed paper purloined from hotels and castles. In them, she beseeched her not to leave her, not to stop loving her, not to shake her off. 'You over-shadowed me like a great mountain that at once uplifted me and awed me.'

Natalie stored these letters in a wooden box. 'Dolly will always have friends,' she wrote of her, 'but they won't be the same friends.' Dolly's letters were desperate with need and insecurity. Her love for Natalie, she said, 'shattered the fortress' of her self-sufficiency:

'You have held so many hands, so many waists, written so many love letters.'
'Always wonderful Natalie, I miss you every night with fierce discomfort . . .'
'Darling Natalie, don't shake me off. Don't stop loving me. You are the only serious thing in my life emotionally.'

---

3 Cocteau and his friends in the avant-garde (Eric Satie, Marie Laurencin, Francis Poulenc), would have evenings of new music, drink, drugs, food and the performance arts. In 1920 a farce by Cocteau, *Le Boeuf sur le Toit*, premièred in Paris.

But Dolly was by no means the only serious thing emotionally in Natalie's life. It was Romaine's letters that were beside Natalie's bed, and when Romaine was in Paris Dolly was ousted. And it was with Romaine that Natalie unswervingly aspired to forge a domestic context.

In 1930 they had a house built to their specification in a pine forest outside Beauvallon, near St Tropez, in the hope of achieving both proximity and independence. They called it the Villa Trait d'Union – the hyphenated villa. It had a shared living room and galleried loggia, but separate front doors, workrooms and bedrooms. It was arranged on the principle of the villa that Natalie had shared with Renée Vivien on Lesbos. The most certain way to lose the one you loved, Natalie said, was to live in passionate intimacy in the same house and the same bed.

In summer, Natalie and Romaine went together to Beauvallon with their respective servants. Natalie entertained her friends – Dolly, Gertrude Stein and Alice B. Toklas, Djuna Barnes, Janet Flanner, Lily de Gramont – while Romaine shut herself in her half of the house and worked on her autobiography, *No Pleasant Memories*, about her mother, and St Mar, and on disturbing pencil drawings which she called introspective patterns imprisoned within encircling lines. 'These drawings should be read. They evolve from the subconscious, without premeditation. They aspire to a maximum of expression with a minimum of means.'

They were images of cruelty and control: a child trying to escape from a woman who holds her by her feet, a figure bound by a devilish force, which she called *Mummy*, reptilian creatures devouring children, which she called *Mother Nature*. There was a girl unable to break free from devils, an idiot chained to an angel, a jester intent on rape, a detached eye shaped like a predatory bird. She signed them with her artist's mark, a wing held down by a chain. Édouard MacAvoy,[4] who in the 1960s painted her portrait, called them 'messages which came from the depths of her nights'.

Romaine could no more stay put at Beauvallon than anywhere else. The proximity of Natalie's guests disturbed her. In the summer of 1933 Natalie visited Arcachon, but letters constantly arrived for her at Beauvallon from Dolly, and a succession of people called there, hoping to see her. They included a tall blonde woman in a car, who did not give her name. Romaine moved to Genoa and wrote Natalie a scathing letter in which she called her weak and governed by vanity. 'Your life at present is infested by rats, <u>& one of these rats is gnawing at the very foundation of our friendship.</u>'

That rat was Dolly.

'As long as you surrounded yourself by a not unfriendly tribe of second-rate young women, though unpleasant, I suffered it to pass.' But now, she said, it was all too much. There were rats in the kitchen, rats in the bedroom, rats in the hall. Unless Natalie cleaned up, and changed everything, there would be no more Romaine.

Natalie, stunned, went into draft after draft of reply. She worked until her words were bleached of all anger. She protested that Dolly was not a rat and voiced concern that Romaine had become increasingly detached from life, but what upset her most about the letter, more than anything Romaine might demand, was the implication that their relationship had become conditional. For her part, nothing

---

4 French portrait painter, professor at the Académie Julian. He depicted Romaine looking like a man. He also drew Natalie on her deathbed.

could alter or corrode the 'pure metal' of her love for Romaine. 'I shall always serve under your near or distant spirit, for all my life remains Romaine.'

Natalie asked to join her in Genoa so that they might talk. Romaine was obdurate. The villa she had rented was cold, the heating insufficient, the steps steep, her Packard could not cope with the hills, she had fired the cook. 'Besides, has Nat Nat bought a nice new broom to sweep up her rooms before leaving?' If not, there could be no visit.

So Natalie bent to Romaine's will. She met Dolly in Paris, told her of Romaine's anxieties, then saw her on to a train for London. Dolly wept the entire journey. 'R might as well insist on your killing me as not to see you,' she wrote. Natalie packed for Genoa. Romaine instructed her to bring tea, haemorrhoid ointment, and *Death Comes for the Archbishop* by Willa Cather.[5]

---

5 Willa Cather (1873–1947), American novelist. *Death Comes for the Archbishop*, her eighth novel, was published in 1927. From 1908 until her death she lived with her friend and travelling companion, Edith Lewis.

19

You phoned and asked me to dinner on Saturday night. We had not spoken for two months. You wanted to talk about our future. You said we should build on what we had and that neither of us was young.

But we had said we were finished, and I had a date on Saturday, Ruth this time. We were to meet at St Paul's station, then walk over the Millennium Bridge to the Tate Modern. Last time, the first time, she had linked her arm through mine.

You said we should make decisions, you used the word commitment. I wondered what you had in mind. Were we to live like my reliable brothers with their reliable wives, silver weddings acknowledged, our wills in the filing cabinet?

I did not know how or what to decide. But I think of us standing in the hallway as we said goodbye. You had on that fur-collared coat, like Oscar Wilde's, and I was naked and you wrapped me into it and held me close, and I thought I could not leave you, that I could not leave you yet.

25

More Dolly Wilde

'I have loved many women, at least I suppose I have.'

Dolly became more bedraggled as drug and alcohol addiction took their course. Without her heroin intake she could not walk, function, or talk lucidly. She was frequently ill with debilitating infections and colds. She attempted detoxifications, cures, psychoanalysis, and reform, but none of it worked. Several times she overdosed, or slashed her wrists in Paris hotels or in rented rooms. In her address book Natalie kept a list of doctors to contact about Dolly's problems. She paid their bills, a commitment she shared with Dolly's friend in London, Pamela Harris,[1] who did not have Natalie's sort of money.

'Honey' Harris supported Dolly through her many crises. If they were lovers, she was too discreet to admit it. Dolly, she thought, had a 'beautiful, kind spirit' and she saw Natalie's influence as destructive. Dolly said of Honey to Natalie, 'She is my Romaine and not to be dealt with roughly.'

[1] In London, Dolly stayed often at the Harris family house at 10 Catherine Street. Honey's grandmother, Mabel Batten, was Radclyffe Hall's 'wife', until usurped by Una Troubridge.

When in 1928 Dolly contracted diphtheria in Venice, it was Honey who went out to her. 'I should have realised,' Dolly wrote to Natalie, 'that Romaine and Lily are the only people you give spiritually to . . . to the others, you give material gifts.'

Dolly wanted to be intrinsic to Natalie's life. In 1929 she tried to find a London publisher for Natalie's ninth book, *The One Who is Legion*, her only work in English. It was a stylistic exercise. Natalie called it an orchestration of inner voices and a study of her views on love.[2] No publisher wanted it. They found it incomprehensible. Natalie paid for 560 copies to be privately printed by Eric Partridge at the Scholaris Press.

Natalie tried to help Dolly, and to balance their tense affair with her relationship with Romaine, her friendships, salon afternoons and her own writing. But Dolly moved beyond spiritual or material help. She added paraldehyde, which she could buy over the counter, to her list of addictive substances. When Natalie had an adventure with an actress in 1931, Dolly threw a wad of bank notes out of the window of the Hotel Astoria in Paris, then attempted suicide.

That same year, Alice Pike Barney died aged seventy-four. On the morning of her death she got up at six, saw her dressmaker, and worked on a play called *Jimmie*, about her friendship with Whistler, which she intended staging in her own theatre, the Theatre Mart. In the early evening she had a bowl of beef broth, then was chauffeured to a concert at the McDowell Town Club. She wore a wig, rings on each finger, a chunky diamond necklace, a velvet hat, a fur coat and high-heeled shoes.

---

2 'It is only by the love we give that we are held. The love we give is the love we want.' Romaine worked with her on the book and did two illustrations for it of emaciated figures floating through the ether.

At the start of the concert she felt faint, moved to a sofa and swooned to her death. She was buried with a simple ceremony near her husband's grave. She had chosen the inscription for her headstone: 'Alice Pike Barney, The Talented One.' Natalie did not feel that death interrupted her relationship with her mother. Until the end of her own life, she said, her mother would remain more alive to her than most of those still living.

Dolly alive was a vexation. There was a difficult correspondence in March 1934 between her legal guardian in London, Tancred Borenius,[3] and Natalie after Dolly cut an artery in her wrist and swallowed sleeping pills. Borenius asked Natalie to take her in and give her a home life. Natalie refused, said it was unfair that Dolly's London friends did not do more, and pointed out that she gave Dolly money. Moreover Dolly had taken drug-addicted friends to 20 rue Jacob when Natalie was away. 'Paris is fatal to her,' Natalie wrote. 'I do not wish to default or fail Dolly in my untiring friendship, but simply ask to be aided and not called upon at the last moment to see her through.'

Dolly wrote to assure her that things were going to be different. 'And we'll spend a happy spring together and forget all this horror . . . Please don't forsake me, ever.'

Romaine went to New York that year, took a suite at the Hotel des Artistes, and began a portrait of Carl Van Vechten.[4] She regretted giving him the finished picture and asked for it back. She also met

---

3 Tancred Borenius (1885–1948), born in Finland, an art historian and managing editor of the *Burlington Magazine* from 1940–5.

4 Carl Van Vechten (1880–1964), writer, artist, photographer and proponent of African-American culture. He was central to the international modernist movement, a big, burly man with a passion for the avant-garde.

up with Gertrude Stein and Alice B. Toklas; Gertrude was on a lecture tour, explaining her own obscure prose. Romaine described her as 'an uneducated Jew' and was dismissive of her views on art.

Romaine sent Natalie newspaper articles about turmoil in Europe, communism, and the vilifying of Jews in Austria and Germany. She hoped Natalie would come to New York and that together they might go to Bermuda and Florida, but she added a swipe at Dolly: 'Of course I always miss Nat Nat, but feel consoled with the idea that she has always had her "confidantes" and bosom friends, notwithstanding my presence.'

Natalie did not join her until April 1935. 'I shall remain in Paris,' she wrote, 'while you rotate according to our different ways of being. Your goings are already too much travel for me.' She had imported a new lover to 20 rue Jacob, Nadine Hwang, who had been a colonel in the Chinese army and then moved to Paris in the early 1930s. Natalie employed her as her chauffeur, secretary, and personal assistant. Dolly was again jealous. Una Troubridge, who saw Dolly at the rue Jacob in 1935, described her as 'haggard and aged by her career of dope'.

Natalie's sexual energy and enthusiasm at the age of sixty impressed monogamous friends like Gertrude Stein and Alice B. Toklas. Alice said Natalie acquired new lovers in the powder rooms of department stores. Nadine Hwang called Natalie her 'darlingest own', and tried to separate her from Dolly who, she claimed, was dealing in opium. She said Dolly had sent a friend to Fontainebleau to collect 300 pounds of it, and had stolen a blue sapphire ring of Natalie's to fund the purchase. Dolly complained to Romaine about 'that *horrible* Chinese' in Natalie's life.

When she was forty-three Dolly was diagnosed with breast cancer.

She refused surgery, described the lumps that grew and multiplied as benign, sought alternative treatments and made a pilgrimage to Lourdes. None of it helped and the cancer metastasised to her lungs. For a while she lived in London in the Kings Road with Gwen Farrar, who was alcoholic. Dolly wrote to Natalie of 'a slovenly impossible atmosphere', a life without discipline, and the constant worry of being in cars driven by someone incapacitated by drink and drugs. Natalie sent silk pyjamas, a handbag and reassurance.

Ten days before Dolly's forty-fourth birthday, on 21 July 1939, Monsieur Toulouse, manager of the Hôtel Montalembert in Paris, wrote to Natalie:

I am told by friends of Miss Wilde that you are the person with the most influence over her. She is drinking so much that delirium tremens will follow and probably suicide. Also, she emits piercing cries all night, alternating with groans which disturb her neighbours. I would be infinitely grateful if you could remove her to a sanatorium.

Natalie and Honey Harris booked her into Chiswick House Nursing Home in London. The matron sent them reports. On 15 August she told Natalie that Dolly had reduced her heroin intake, cut out whisky and was drinking only lager. Restraint did not last. By October, Dolly was in the Basil Street Hotel, drinking and taking drugs, running up bills and imploring Natalie to come to her. A fortnight before she died, a Dr Robert LeMasle knocked at Berthe Cleyrergue's apartment in the rue Jacob and told her he was back from London where he had chanced on Dolly, drunk and unconscious, on a bench in Westminster Square.

Cancer spread to her uterus and in April 1940 Dr Douglas Macauley of the Chiswick nursing home wrote to Natalie that treatment could only be palliative. Dolly killed herself on 9 April 1941 with paraldehyde and heroin in rented rooms in Chesham Place. London was being bombed. She described her life as a vicious circle of pain and sterility: 'I see something, I can't express it.' She was destroyed by addiction, as was her alcoholic father, Willie, Oscar Wilde's brother. She was buried on 15 April 1941 at Kensal Green Cemetery.

Natalie avoided funerals. She was caustic about the pointlessness of 'trailing after empty coats', or of 'calling on friends who were out'. Like Gertrude Stein she believed that dead is dead. Her tribute to her lovers was to endeavour to keep them alive through their work. Ten years after Dolly's death, she privately published *In Memory of Dorothy Ierne Wilde: Oscaria*, printed by Darantière Press and paid for by herself. On the frontispiece she showed a photo of Dolly dressed as Oscar with slicked-back hair and a cravat.

In Memory was an anthology in English and French of tributes from friends. Honey Harris wrote of Dolly's charm and her sorrowful walk. Alice B. Toklas remarked on her 'almost mythical pristine freshness in 1916 – that alas became a bit tarnished', and Gertrude Stein said of her, 'Well, she certainly hadn't a fair run for her money.' Janet Flanner described her as 'utterly singular and unique'. She had, she said, 'as many versions of herself, all as slightly different, as could have been seen in views of her supplied by a room lined with mirrors'. Lily de Gramont wrote of her Irish beauty, impertinence, social charm and her 'extraordinary verbal gift, inherited from her famous uncle, that was nourished by everything she heard and saw'. She compared her to a runner who could never run fast enough, a gambler for whom the stakes were never high enough. She died, she said, '*encore jeune, encore belle, encore avide*': 'still young, still beautiful, still eager'.

Natalie wove her way among such tributes, much as she did with guests at her salon. It was she whom Dolly had loved and she made that clear by including in the published book some of Dolly's letters to her. She wanted to save Dolly from oblivion, give her the book she never had the discipline to write, and ally her with her uncle Oscar's wit, writing talent, and same-sex desires.

20

My blind date nicked the cash from my wallet – about eighty quid, the gold chain you gave me, and my pass for the underground. I was glad she wanted to see me again. She suggested supper at my flat. I told her to look around while I sorted things in the kitchen. I thought she would like to browse my bookshelves. We ate brie and olives, drank red wine. She said flattering things, then after kissing and more she was gone. She said she must get back to her daughter, but left me her phone number. Or so I thought.

In the morning I supposed I would find the chain in the bedclothes. Or perhaps it had come unclasped in the pool. When I went to collect my dry cleaning, I had no cash. When I dialled her number I got a haulage service. What next, I wonder. Free love can test your nerve.

26

Ladies Almanack

*'My love is a selfish, glorious, god-like thing. It has moments
of genius. She generally sleeps through these.'*

Djuna Barnes[1] wrote *Ladies Almanack* at Natalie's suggestion in
March and April 1928. It was an outrageous satire on Natalie and
her circle, full of references to sexual technique, furrows, nooks,
whorls, crevices, and wild behaviour, a manual for lesbians who
'discard Duster, Offspring and Spouse'.

Irreligious and scathing, mystifying to those who could not
fathom its references, and hilarious to those who could decode
and understand it, it was an insiders' spoof that parodied contemporary sexology. It was audacious, subversive, innovative in style
and a contrast to Radclyffe Hall's *The Well of Loneliness*, which had
been banned in London in the same year. The editor of the *Sunday
Express*, James Douglas, in a leading article, wrote that he would
rather give his daughter a phial of prussic acid than let her read

---

1 Djuna Chappell Barnes (1892–1982) left America in 1921 for Paris. She was sent there
as a journalist by McCall's magazine.

Radclyffe Hall's chaste *Well*.[2] Had the *Almanack* appeared in London, neither he, the Lord Chancellor, nor the Director of Public Prosecutions, would have understood it. Like Virginia Woolf's *Orlando*,[3] also published in London in 1928, which was about and dedicated to Vita Sackville-West, the lesbian allusions were too cryptic and the style too clever for them to feel disturbed.

Djuna Barnes constructed the *Almanack* like a medieval calendar with monthly entries and zodiac signs that corresponded to some aspect of desire – the 'twining thigh', the 'seeking arm'. Lesbians were not failed men, inadequate women, or some 'third sex'. They had wicked fun. In the unhappy *Well*, Natalie was cast as Valerie Seymour, a good-intentioned lesbian who gave courage to her dismal sisters in their overwhelming tragedy of 'inversion'. In the *Almanack*, she was Dame Evangeline Musset, a lesbian pope, whose desires were infinite and whose bed was never empty. When Dame Musset died aged ninety-nine, forty women shaved their heads, carried her corpse through the streets of Paris, sealed her in a tomb for a while then laid her on a funeral pyre. She burned to ash, except for her tongue – it 'flamed and would not suffer Ash and it played about'. Her acolytes sat on it and 'from under their Skirts a slow Smoke issued'. They took the immortal tongue in an urn and put it on an altar in her temple of love, 'where it flickers to this day'.

After such a death Dame Musset was sanctified. Barnes accorded her a saint's day for every month, each commemorating a decade of her life. April celebrated how 'When fast on fifteen she hushed

2 'I would rather give a healthy boy or a healthy girl a phial of prussic acid than this novel. Poison kills the body, but moral poison kills the soul' (19 August 1928).

3 Virginia Woolf (1882–1941), English novelist, compulsive letter writer, and a key figure in the Bloomsbury Group. *Orlando* was an elaborate love letter to Vita Sackville-West.

a Near-Bride with the left Flounce of her Ruffle that her Father
in sleeping might not know of the Oh!' June was in honour of
how 'when thirty she like all Men before her, made a Harlot a
good Woman by making her Mistress'.

The language was a mix of ornate Elizabethan and colloquial
English, with many capital letters, neologisms, cryptic allusions
and dirty jokes. Dolly Wilde was Doll Furious, or Doll on her
Arm, or 'my great big beautiful bedridden Doll':

> 'And' said Dame Musset, rising in Bed, 'that's all
> there is, and there is no more.'
> 'But oh!' cried Doll.
> 'Down Woman,' said Dame Musset in her friendliest,
> 'there may be a mustard seed!'
> 'A grain, a grain!' lamented Doll.

The July entry told of how Dame Musset and Doll Furious planned
their meetings to avoid their menstrual cycles – information Natalie
had given to Djuna.

The only non-lesbian in the book was Djuna's friend, the poet
Mina Loy.[4] She appeared as Patience Scalpel, determined that her
daughters 'shall go a'marrying'. In real life Mina Loy would not
let her daughter, Joella, go to Natalie's salon out of fear that Natalie
would seduce her.

Janet Flanner and her partner Solita Solana were Nip and Tuck,
breezy journalists. Romaine, Dame Musset's final choice in love,

---

4 Mina Loy (1882–1966) moved to Paris from England in 1923. Primarily a poet, she
also wrote plays, painted, designed lampshades, and acted.

was Cynic Sal who wore a top hat, cracked a sharp whip, and 'never once descended the Driver's seat to put her Head within'. Lily de Gramont was the Duchesse Clitoressa of Natescourt, who often took tea with the Dame. Una Troubridge was Lady Buck-and-Balk who 'sported a Monocle and believed in Spirits'. Radclyffe Hall was Tilly Tweed-in-Blood, who 'sported a Stetson and believed in Marriage' – but only between women. One was to be a wife, the other a bride. They appeared in March and involved them-selves with questions of sexual fidelity and legal rights. Mimi Franchetti was Senorita Fly-About.[5]

The *Almanack* was privately published by Robert McAlmon[6] and printed in Dijon, by Darantière Press. Djuna herself hand-coloured the illustrations in about forty copies. She feared confis-cation by the postal service if she had page proofs delivered to her own address, so she asked Sylvia Beach to take them at her book-shop. Sylvia declined. References to lesbian 'Fore Parts', 'burning Quarters' and 'the Consolation every Woman has at her Finger Tips, or at the very Hang of her Tongue', made her foresee trouble with the authorities of the sort she received when she published *Ulysses* in 1922.

Robert McAlmon's money came from his wife Winifred Ellerman, 'Bryher', whose father, Sir John Ellerman, the richest man in Britain, owned the shipping company, Ellerman Lines, and most of the shares in *The Times*, *Illustrated London News*, *Sphere*, *Tatler*, and *Sketch*. Bryher took her name from one of the Scilly Isles. She was

---

5 She had a brief affair with Natalie and, in 1935, invited Una Troubridge to 'have a little scandal'.

6 Robert McAlmon (1896–1956). Born in Kansas, he specialised in books 'not likely to be published, for commercial or legislative reasons'.

the lover of the American imagist poet Hilda Doolittle, known as H.D., who wrote that Bryher loved her 'so madly it is terrible. No man has ever cared for me like that.'[7]

Bryher met McAlmon, who was homosexual and an impoverished writer, in America in 1921. She suggested they marry as a lavender cover-up. She would give him an allowance: they could live separate lives, have their same-sex lovers and join up for occasional visits to her parents. They married on St Valentine's Day and *The Times* headline was 'Heiress weds unknown'. In his memoir, *Being Geniuses Together,* McAlmon wrote: 'We neither of us felt the slightest attraction towards each other, but remained perfectly friendly.'

Bryher, H.D. and McAlmon sailed together for Paris. There, and with Bryher's funds and editorial help, he set up, at 29 Quai d'Anjou, the Contact Publishing Company and *Contact* magazine, which between 1922 and 1930 published, in many cases for the first time, Ernest Hemingway, Gertrude Stein, Ezra Pound, H.D., Djuna Barnes, Mina Loy and James Joyce. Bryher herself was a friend and benefactor of Sylvia Beach and kept Shakespeare and Company solvent. She also subsidised Harriet Weaver's Egoist Press in London, which published Joyce's *Portrait of the Artist as a Young Man.* While she travelled with H.D. in Italy, Greece and Switzerland, her parents thought she was with McAlmon in Paris.

Like many others, Djuna Barnes had a brief affair with Natalie, but the love of her life was Thelma Wood, a silverpoint artist[8]

---

7 Bryher (1894–1983) paid for all H.D.'s medical care when after the birth of her daughter Perdita, she had a prolonged depression.

8 Silverpoint is a slow, meticulous drawing technique, that gives tonal subtlety, using sharpened silver wire in a stylus on specially coated paper.

from St Louis who drank excessively and had casual sex with countless partners, one of whom was Edna St Vincent Millay. She and Djuna shared a flat near the Café Aux Deux Magots. Djuna wanted fidelity. 'I was never a lesbian, I only loved Thelma Wood,'[9] she said of herself with no particular accuracy. Thelma, she believed, wanted her 'and the rest of the world'.

While Djuna was writing the *Almanack*, Thelma was in the process of leaving her for another woman, Henriette Metcalf.[10] In despair, Djuna then in 1936 wrote *Nightwood*, 'A soul talking to itself in the heart of the night', about their eight-year relationship. She read the typescript to Thelma who said it proved Djuna did not understand her, was insulted by it, hit her in the mouth and threw a cup of tea at her.

Djuna dedicated the *Almanack* to Thelma and used the money it earned to pay hospital bills when Thelma injured her spine. She did not put her own name to it, the author was simply 'A Lady of Fashion'. She smuggled copies into America; in Paris she hawked them among friends and sold them through Edward Titus at his Black Manikin bookshop in the rue Delambre.[11]

The first edition of 1,000 copies sold out within days. Plain editions cost $10: signed and coloured ones $50. Janet Flanner thought Djuna Barnes the most important woman writer in Paris. Natalie was more than pleased to be Dame Musset, and loved the

---

9 Quoted in Hank O'Neal's *Life is painful, nasty and short . . .* (New York, Paragon House, 1990).

10 Henriette McCrea Metcalf (1888–1981), wealthy and twice married, was a friend of Colette's and translated *La Dame aux Camélias* into English. She believed in God, astrology, psychic phenomena, and in helping animals and the unfortunate.

11 Titus started his bookshop with money from his wife, Helena Rubinstein. He cheated Djuna Barnes into putting his name on the title page as if he was the publisher and also into giving him a cut of the profits.

book for its wit and subversiveness. She wrote to Dolly that she laughed herself sick over it. It gave her a lifelong respect for Djuna's work, and in later years when Djuna was hard up she offered her a monthly allowance so that she could afford to go on writing.

21

In a tight dress of black brocade, Shirley posed by a pillar. Her hands and Adam's apple looked incongruous. She jutted her hips and arched her back: in high heels her large feet hurt.

She was suing Barnham Institute, alleging sexual discrimination. Her tutor, Ms Macaulay, asked her to discontinue Beauty Bag classes. Her sister students tolerated her through make-up, skin care and minor blemishes, but took against her on the bikini-line depilation evening. They complained, walked out and said if she did not go, they would.

She was a reputable chartered accountant, her divorce was civilised, and she paid maintenance to her wife and sons. She had weekly counselling with a licensed psychotherapist and had impressed her doctors with her resolve and ability to function in her chosen gender.

Oestrogen therapy had atrophied her testicles. She was proud of her bosom and her bottom, which both became quite large. She spent a fortune on electrolysis. She wanted to have her penis reconstructed to create a clitoris and her trachea shaved to lighten her voice.

She had a passion for fashion, interior design, and cooking. Given her painful and unwavering commitment to self-realisation, she told me it seemed to her worse than unfair to ban her from the Beauty Bag because her knickers bulged.

27

A War Interlude

'Hard times cannot last for ever.'

The Second World War imposed late proximity on Natalie and Romaine. Six years and a day was the span of their enforced intimacy. They were together for the bread ration in the morning and for tinned stew at night. They endured each other's intransigent personalities: Romaine's daunting egocentricity, Natalie's compulsive sociability. Neither took easily to the need for compromise that shared life prescribed. Each felt separated from her bedrock of identity: Romaine, without paints, was denied her 'artist self'. Natalie lost enlightenment: her salon life, and her adventures of heart and mind.

In 1940 Natalie was sixty-four, her 'darling angel' two years younger. Three years before the war, Romaine had turned her back on Paris and moved to the villa Sant' Agnese, in the hills above Florence, with Antonio her cook and manservant, and a couple of maids. Her villa had an adjoining farm and an old-fashioned garden.

Romaine had become most peculiar: hypochondriacal, paranoid and disdainful. She imagined she was going blind and hoarded trunks of medicines out of fear of wartime shortages. She was bitter that her line drawings, which she called her most intimate expression, had been ignored, and that her autobiography, *No Pleasant Memories*, was unacceptable to any publisher.

It seemed inconceivable to her that Britain and France could go to war with Italy, the country whose beauty she loved and whose culture she respected. She believed in a master race of Aryans,[1] and had an obsessive fear of Bolshevik invasion and rule by the peasantry.

She admired Mussolini's force and statuesque figure,[2] and liked the displays of the fascisti: the piazzas filled with militia, with 10,000 daggers raised in salute, flashing in the sunlight. She had grieved when D'Annunzio died on 1 March 1938. Italy designated a day of national mourning: his body lay in state and his lakeside farmhouse, the Vittoriale, with its temple, theatre, and parkland, was bequeathed to the Italian nation.

Natalie, in Paris when hostilities began, was more personally horrified by the prospect of war. It threatened to destroy much that she cherished: her Friday salons, summers in Beauvallon with Romaine and at Honfleur with Lily, her love affairs, mornings spent writing, afternoon tea with Colette, Berthe's excellent cooking, evening walks round Paris with Gertrude Stein and her large white poodle, Basket:

Gertrude's staunch presence, the pleasant touch of hand, the well-rounded voice always ready to chuckle. Our talks and walks

1 'If the Jew were not washed by the Aryan, he would not be able to see out of his eyes for filth,' Hitler said in 1941.
2 Benito Mussolini (1883–1945), fascist dictator, declared war on Britain and France on 10 June 1940.

led us far from war paths. Wandering in our quiet old quarter, we fell comfortably into thought and step. Basket, unleashed, ran ahead, a white blur, the ghost of a dog in the moonlit streets.

When the quiet old quarter became a war zone, Gertrude, Alice and Basket moved to the country house they rented in Bilignin, in the Rhône Valley. It was a time of separations. Dolly saw Natalie on to the train for Florence then left for London by the last boat train. Natalie spoke of being haunted by the twitch in her smile as they waved goodbye. They did not see each other again.

Florence was full of German soldiers. Romaine called them blond warriors keeping the Red Russians at bay. Hitler, she thought, was a scapegoat to conceal the Bolshevik plan of a world revolution that would destroy old class structures and consign to oblivion the works of Shakespeare, Dante, Petrarch, Galileo, Michelangelo and herself.

Her neighbours in nearby villas were countesses or Americans who had married into the Italian aristocracy. Jews she viewed as troublemakers.[3] She sacked her gardener, saying he was a communist thief who lived with communist cronies in a jerry-built house of the sort that was spoiling Florence. She was sure it was they who had shouted under her window at night, '*Abasso i signori*' ('Down with the proprietors').

Natalie's arrival brought familiarity and reassurance, but problems too. She felt marooned in wartime Florence and cut off from friends. Bombing raids scared her witless and her Italian was poor. Bernard Berenson, who confessed he had been in love with her when young,

---

3 Hitler viewed them as Colorado beetles (*Kartoffelkafer*) or bacteria. 'They must be treated like tuberculosis bacilli from which a healthy body can become infected.'

temporarily abandoned his nearby home, villa I Tatti, for refuge in Switzerland, taking his books and paintings with him.[4] Natalie hoped she and Romaine might also find safe harbour there, but doubted they would get the necessary permissions to cross the frontier.

And Romaine's moods proved daunting. When visited by an Austrian-Jewish neighbour, who had married an Italian, she shut herself in her bedroom until he was gone, then 'descended on Natalie like a thunderstorm' telling her their situation demanded caution. When Natalie later loaned him their cook for an evening, Romaine told her she was borrowing from Peter to pay Paul, that she, Romaine, was Peter and that Paul was any stranger Natalie happened to meet round any corner.

They disagreed over who should instruct the servants. Romaine accused Natalie of creating complications, then leaving her to sort out the mess. She said Natalie always wanted the windows cleaned, or the pond emptied, when there was no one to do it, and expected the household to be run efficiently when there were now only motley staff and grim rations.

Berthe, Natalie's housekeeper, stayed in Paris throughout the war. Natalie missed her, and kept her busy with written instructions: to send hairnets and Renée Vivien's poems, to pack in camphor the tapestry De Montesquiou had given her, to find and forward Dolly's will, to go round to 67 rue Raynouard and help Lily de Gramont, to send news of Lucie Delarue-Mardrus's health and welfare,[5] to

4 Barbara Berenson (1865–1959). American art critic and historian. His villa I Tatti, famous for its library, art collection, and gardens, was his home for sixty years.

5 Lucie Delarue-Mardrus was in her late sixties and suffering from rheumatism. She had no money and was living in a house in Château-Gontier in Normandy with her current lover, the opera singer Germaine de Castro, who was wanted by the Gestapo.

ensure that the ivy in the garden of 20 rue Jacob was well maintained.

Natalie viewed such Italian maids as they could find as inadequate substitutes for Berthe. She nagged them. 'Nag she must, and all the time,' Romaine said. By way of reprisal, one maid failed properly to store Natalie's fur coat and winter clothes, so moths got at them.

Bombs dropped in nearby roads. Air-raid sirens sounded every few hours so they scurried to a shelter, huddled in the cellar, or crouched in a sewer that ran through adjacent fields. All such cover seemed inadequate to Romaine, so she arranged for a trench to be dug in the garden.

Because of their money, class and American citizenship, they thought it dangerous to go out, and they were suspicious of all young men they saw. When buying a pair of scissors in Florence, in April 1941, Natalie was asked by the shopkeeper if she was German; she said she was American, he shook his head and told her she was destroying his country and killing its women.

Natalie felt she had moved from a city of light to occupation and destruction on a scale that seemed like devilry. Primarily she viewed the enemy as man, who could not love enough. She thought all war benighted, and a male perversity. Romaine, more fascistic, feared the enemy within, the swarthy-skinned farmhand, the gardener, the plumber.

There were no quiet days or nights. In one raid a baby was blasted into their fields and its clothes dangled from a bush. The window glass of the villa was blown out, they could hear hand grenades being thrown in the street, Natalie thought a bomb had been flung through the broken gratings of their cellar. Someone painted a huge hammer and sickle with VIVA STALIN in red on their roof; they supposed it was done by Bolshevik workmen as an invitation to the fascists or to the English to drop a bomb on them. They each kept a small case packed with soap, comb, toothbrush and bedbug powder for when the communists came to arrest them. They hid trunks and boxes of possessions in unlikely places, though they were not sure from whom, and they listened at all hours to the wireless, but formed no coherent idea of what was going on. When Mussolini was imprisoned in the mountains in July 1943 after a revolt in his own Council, Romaine called it the end of all hope of a united Europe; she was relieved when Hitler sent German paratroops to free him.

It was not the life they were used to and it took its toll. Romaine said her artist's soul was in revolt. She had nightmares and groaned in her sleep, waking Natalie who would go to her room to console her. Natalie felt that life, as she understood it, had come to a stop. She had angina, she was unable to hoist herself on to the trams and had to be shoved from the back by Romaine. She kept falling and hurting her knees and Romaine would put witch-hazel compresses on them. Crouched at night in the trench in the garden in her fur coat, covered with stones and mud, with bomber planes flying low, Natalie expected death in a grave already dug. As lights from bombs rained down over Florence she kept up a chatter about how the gardener had planted out the lilies from the greenhouse far too soon and neglected the magnolia tree, which was consequently losing its leaves. Romaine wished for a bunker where Natalie would hear nothing of the raids. 'I am sure it is the noise, more than anything that affects her,' she said.

They were shocked to hear of the bombing of Siena and Tivoli, and of the cathedral and old library at Rouen. 'Are all the old palaces and monuments the world over to be destroyed by this war?' Romaine wrote. 'Palaces and monuments created in those times when Aryan geniuses, like giants, led the way.' From Berthe, Natalie heard that Paris was going through a similar nightmare. Bomb damage had destroyed the roof of 20 rue Jacob and felled the chestnut tree in the garden. When German soldiers threatened to occupy the house, Berthe warned them off by saying that Natalie was a close friend of Mussolini's.

Food in Florence became scarce. The cost of eggs rose from five to forty lire each. Natalie and Romaine's rations were meagre tins of stew and half a pound of bread a day. They lived off vegetables from Romaine's farm, Antonio's corned beef prepared with a special kind of salt, and rabbits shot by Tomalino, the gardener. By September 1943 they had no electricity, gas or water, except from the garden cistern. 'We aren't living any more, we are surviving,' Natalie wrote to Berthe. On Thanksgiving Day, 23 November, they ate Tomalino's pet turkey, though he was loath to kill it; they had it with potato chips and fried pumpkin. On Christmas Day, neighbours came in and they all drank Asti Spumante and ate walnut cake. Natalie gave Romaine a black and white wooden box, Romaine gave Natalie a microscope.

Natalie rued the lack of hot water. 'Inconveniences of this sort make her angry,' Romaine wrote. 'She is spoilt. She has never known what real want means, and for her sake I hope the war will never oblige us to face it.' For herself, she believed she was inured to hardship. 'Poverty is an old acquaintance of mine,' she wrote. She liked often to reiterate how for seven years in Paris she had lived on a precarious pittance, without winter clothes, in a fireless studio, and in worn shoes had trudged the cold and muddy streets warmed by the inner fire of art.

From time to time they were questioned by fascist officials. Good-looking young men arrived on motorcycles wearing knee-breeches and long black boots. Romaine and Natalie told them they had been friends with D'Annunzio and Mussolini, that they loved Italy, hoped for a Europe without war or famine, and were artists who abhorred politics. After the young men left, they feared they might have said something incriminating and would be sent to a concentration camp.

As the allies advanced, Natalie and Romaine's fascist sympathies were of no help to them. There was shelling from the incoming British and the departing Germans. In July 1944 Tomalino and his family turned against them, armed themselves with agricultural implements and refused to hand over any of the wheat, olive oil and potatoes, farmed from Romaine's land. They said the land belonged to them and that they would crush Antonio's ribs if they found him in their zucchini patch.

Natalie and Romaine ventured into Florence for help. They were shocked to see the Ponte Vecchio badly damaged. It was as if with the destruction of bridges across the Arno, past connections went too. By chance they met Martha Gellhorn,[6] Ernest Hemingway's wife, who was dressed in khaki and wearing a war-reporter's badge. She took them to a British army major; they told him how the peasants in their employment were occupying their farm, menacing them with scythes and pitchforks and denying

6 Martha Gellhorn (1908–98). She left Hemingway after five years. She reported on the Nuremberg trial of Adolf Eichmann and was a correspondent for the *Atlantic Monthly* as well as writing five novels.

them their own produce. The major sent soldiers to arrest Tomalino, his father, and his brother; all three were imprisoned for possessing firearms.

On 31 August 1944 Natalie and Romaine returned from the shelter after an air raid to find their house full of soldiers from the retreating German army, writing letters, browsing through their books, and firing a large cannon in the garden. There was a flute-playing captain and a colonel with a great dane. After two days they moved on, leaving the whole place in a mess, and taking livestock and produce with them.

When the Germans surrendered in April 1945, Natalie made an American flag from a white sheet, a red silk dressing gown and blue pyjamas. In Milan, Mussolini was shot by a firing squad and his body hung upside down in a public square. In Florence the streets filled with soldiers, people moved handcarts of furniture out of hiding, bicycles were sequestered, partisans were told to disband and give up arms, and Natalie befriended a large English policeman on the Ponte Trinità.

Natalie hurried around Florence to secure safe passage out of Italy for herself and Romaine. She saw lawyers, the Swiss Consul, the manager of the Monte dei Paschi Bank. Romaine followed, trying to keep in view the white dots on Natalie's blue silk dress. Natalie longed for Paris but was afraid 'after all these arrested years'. Such friends as were still alive were booking 'very doubtful passages back home'. Dolly was dead. Una was in London alone as Radclyffe Hall had died of cancer. Gertrude Stein was mortally ill in France.

Natalie returned to Paris alone on 24 May 1946. She instructed Berthe to meet her at the Gare de Lyon at seven in the morning: 'I will need some spring dresses: the black taffetas made by Worth

in 1940, hats, shoes, and all you can think of that I will need.'
She intended to go to Laura's apartment at 74 rue Raynouard while
20 rue Jacob was being repaired and prepared.

Romaine stayed in Italy. 'The war is now over,' she wrote in her
diary. 'Natalie has departed for Paris. I miss her very much. I
remain alone seeking to find the other, the artist self that has
deserted me during these years of war on the hills of Florence.'

22

When your ceiling fell in and you moved, out of convenience, into my small flat, we managed all right for many months. We were happy eating together and watching carnage on television. I supposed it was like being married. I was sad when you left, but glad to have back silence, loneliness, and again to feel free to stew my own apples.

28

Tenuous Freedoms

'I want to be the bow, the arrow and the target.'

Natalie was seventy when she returned to a Paris of austerity and food rationing. She found it hard to adjust to separation from Romaine, the loss of lovers and friends, the damage to her home. Her house needed a new roof and windows. The floor of the Temple of Friendship had subsided. Janet Flanner said of the war, 'With the material destruction collapsed invisible things that lived within it.'

Natalie suggested to Romaine that they set up home together in Paris in these changed and uncertain times. Romaine rejected the idea with her usual stark refrain: she missed Nat Nat in a big sense, they would see each other often, but she was an artist so had to be alone. She reiterated how she loathed Paris and said she did not want her villa in Florence to be 'a nest of worries overrun by a band of horrible people.'

'I wonder why you are taking so much to heart my desire to get back to my painting and painter's life,' she asked, and surmised that it was because for the first time ever Natalie was free from the 'double distraction' of another lover. There was, she said, a downstairs room always available for Nat Nat in her house, but her own solitude was essential.

Natalie, in reply, apologised for being an erotic debauchee, thanked Romaine for her beauty, said the nearness of the flesh was an illusion and the nearness of the mind a delight, and admitted to feeling lonely without her angel. From 1946 she missed, too, her evening walks round Paris with Gertrude Stein and wrote a valediction to her. She befriended Alice B. Toklas, who was widowed beyond consolation. Nor would there again be walks with Lily de Gramont, enfeebled by ill health and the death of a daughter. Natalie accompanied her to Evian and Fontainebleau to take the waters and a cure.

Those she had loved belonged to a brighter time. In the decade after the war her Friday salon lost its optimism and candour. Liane de Pougy died in a Swiss convent in 1950. Eva Palmer, 'the mother of my desires, the initiator of my joys', died in Greece in June 1952. The 'precious life-giving habit' of going to see Colette, ended in 1954. Lily de Gramont died that same year. She and Natalie had afternoon tea together on 24 October: Lily left in the early evening and died in the night. Natalie took a basket of white lilac and lilies to the rue Raynouard and placed it by her body.

She served the memory of those she had loved and tried to keep their work alive. She published *In Memory of Dorothy Ierne Wilde: Oscaria* in 1951, established and funded the Prix Renée Vivien to honour women poets writing in French, devoted a Friday salon to Eva Palmer, and published *Nos secrets amours* – Lucie Delarue-Mardrus's poems about her love for Natalie. 'I don't suppose you want a copy of such a past. Of mine. All in passionate verse,' she wrote to Romaine. Romaine did not.

A sense of life's transience made Natalie ever more protective of Romaine. She proved her love in all that she did to please her. Though she disliked practicalities, she prepared Romaine's Paris apartment so it could be rented out: she supervised the decorating, chose the tenants and mediated with Laura about Romaine's securities, shares and trust accounts and what bonds she should buy. She put pictures in store, auctioned large pieces of furniture, arranged a *camion* to take to Nice and Florence the things Romaine wanted, including a Monet painting, and sent her, as requested, blackcurrant lozenges, molasses, scarf pins, Lifebuoy soap with which she liked to wash her hair, details of an anti-flu vaccine, and newly published books like *The Grass Harp* by Truman Capote[1] and Katherine Mansfield's *Letters*.[2] She advised Romaine to get an oil change for her Studebaker[3] and to pour strong disinfectant down the bath plughole.

Natalie arranged that if Romaine were to fall ill or die, her servants should contact her and no one else. She made Romaine the main beneficiary of her will. 'No one is as busy over your affairs as I am,' she wrote. Only rarely did she say, with passing irritation, that she could not go and find Romaine's favoured elephant paper[4] that day, or declare herself 'fussed and harassed by

---

1 Truman Capote (1924–84), Natalie had liked his first novel, *Other Voices Other Rooms*, published in 1948, about a boy growing up in the Deep South who has a relationship with a transvestite. She was less keen on *The Grass Harp* first published in 1951. 'I'm afraid he's a one-book boy', she wrote to Romaine.

2 Katherine Mansfield (1888–1923), New Zealand-born short-story writer. She had a life-long intense friendship with a college friend, Ida Baker. Aged 20, she moved to London and in 1918 married the editor and writer John Middleton Murry. She too admired Oscar Wilde: 'risk, risk everything,' she wrote to Murry. She died of tuberculosis.

3 Romaine had a 1950 bullet-nose saloon. The last Studebaker was produced in 1966.

4 28 × 23 inch drawing paper. It may have had a watermark of an elephant, as used in some Dutch and German papers from the seventeenth century onwards.

so much to do'. She wished Romaine all health, love, and quiet, and hoped her will to work and play would surface soon.

Natalie accepted that only when alone did Romaine have a true sense of identity, and yet, she said, a sigh escaped from her as she remembered the days when they lay close together by the lilac trees in the Bois de Boulogne. 'Thy will be done not mine, my angel and ever all love from Nat Nat,' she wrote. She tried to entice Romaine to visit her, join her for holidays, or travel with her. She tried, too, to tempt her with the simple pleasures of life. From the Grand Hôtel du Parc in Evian, she wrote to her of the excellent *poulets de beurre* and *gigot* and of the joy of tea in the apple orchard. Romaine resisted: 'For me making plans is the enemy of work.' She suffered from sinusitis, bladder problems and indigestion: though she chewed each mouthful of food many times, her throat still constricted when she tried to swallow. Gino, her new cook and manservant, had to pound her on the back. 'Freud said one must not travel if one is not master of one's bowels. He had an awful time with his.' As did she.

So Natalie continued with kind letters, no expectations, and unconditional love. She worked to prepare a catalogue of Romaine's paintings and drawings, and again and again pressed publishers to take her autobiography *No Pleasant Memories*. Somerset Maugham agreed to read it and Natalie also sent it to Max White at *Harpers* in New York. Maugham thought a less dismal title might help: *Autobiography of an American Abroad* perhaps. White's criticism was harsh: Romaine's political views were distasteful and invalidated her other opinions, the organisation of the book was faulty, diary entries for the war years were in an entirely different style from earlier reminiscences, she was overly discreet and obfuscating with her use of initials instead of naming people. 'It would be a great mistake to submit the book for publication as it stands,' he said. 'It would make more enemies among editors than friends.'

Natalie sent his comments to Romaine, whose response was that she now no longer cared whether the thing was published or not. Her concerns narrowed to her own comfort and isolation. In Florence she moved from the Villa Sant' Agnese to the Villa Gaia, then bought another nearby villa, La Chiocciola (the snail), with views of lemon trees and flowers, to use as a studio. She changed its staircase, and replaced the doors and windows. She also bought a flat in Nice, in the rue des Ponchettes, in the old town. She told Natalie to give no one her addresses for she wanted no visitors.

On warm afternoons in Nice, Gino would wait while Romaine sat in the sun on a bench by the shore, then he drove her home and cooked her something plain, like a chop, for her solitary supper. Her hope was that the vacuum she had contrived might lead to personal expression, but in reality she was depressed and seemed to be her mother's victim. She complained of the monotony of her daily life and of how she felt half alive. 'My dead mother gets between me and life. I act as she commands. To me she is the root enemy of all things.'

She had no interest in past friendships. Ida Rubinstein settled in nearby Vence in 1945 and many times suggested to Romaine that they again meet. Romaine always declined. 'I suppose an artist must live alone and feel free otherwise all individuality goes. I can think of my painting only when alone, even less do any actual work,' she wrote. But however much she thought, no work got done. She sat on her solitary bench by the sea, ate her modest meals, suspected that 'awful looking Orientals' were communists, and seemed closed to the world.

'One must be careful only to know people who live more or less like oneself,' she told Natalie. 'You are different from me. You belong to a milieu that appreciated you. You must have your dose of people of your sort which are not my sort . . . I live for months alone, completely, and perforce like it.'

Romaine agreed to or declined the meetings Natalie so wanted. If arrangements did not please Romaine, Natalie suffered. In spring 1954 Natalie booked her into the Meurice hotel, near the rue Jacob. Romaine described it as worse than a prison and she hated Paris: 'the mud, the dirt and bad air, and nowhere to park the car'. Later in the year Natalie did better. At the Continental, Romaine's room had a balcony and bathroom, and it overlooked the Tuileries. Natalie's car met her from the station, her trunk was attended to. 'So glad my angel is with her ever devoted and all loving Nat Nat.'

At ease with herself, Natalie lazed in her hammock in the garden, took massages and cures, and watched her health, particularly her weight and high blood pressure. She worked on a new anthology of *pensées*: *Le Carquois de l'Amazone*, and an eclectic memoir, *Souvenirs Indiscrets*. She gave hours of interviews to a potential biographer, Renée Lang,[5] but then imposed so many constraints that the project floundered. She maintained old connections and forged new ones. Ezra Pound's son, Omar Shakespear Pound,[6] turned up at one of her salons. Alice B. Toklas suggested another possible publisher for Romaine's unpleasant *Memories*. Natalie took

---

5 Renée Lang had published a book on André Gide and was working at the time on a life of Rainer Maria Rilke.

6 Poet and translator of Arabic and Persian texts. His mother was Dorothy Shakespear.

Truman Capote to Romaine's deserted studio where her portraits were stored, and told him of the personalities and relationships of Ida Rubinstein, Lily de Gramont, Una Troubridge, and Gluck. He described it as 'the all-time ultimate gallery of famous dykes'; they formed, he said, 'an international daisy chain'.

Natalie wanted to protect Romaine's 'excessive sensibility, her artist's nature'. She offered all she had: she would live with her, drop everything to help her, do anything for her. But she discovered, yet again, that she could not persuade those whom she loved and desired to make their lives into a work of art in the affirmative way she envisaged. She could not change the essential Romaine, live her life for her, or put right all that was more than wrong.

Visiting her in Florence or Nice was fraught with difficulties. Romaine worried about which bed Natalie should have, whether she would make demands on the servants, how she would cope with spiders in the cupboards, ants in the garden, and scorpions with white legs. She suggested in July 1955 that Natalie stay at the Excelsior, in Florence, and that they meet up in the afternoons. Natalie did not want to be alone in a hotel, in the heat of summer: 'If my room in your villa is no longer available,' she wrote, 'why not reserve for me the one you like at the nearby *pension* – say from July 25th until August 15th which would give us three weeks together.' Romaine conceded and let her stay, but it was a strain for them both: Natalie ate too quickly, talked too much, expected too much of Gino, was too social. 'My angel's weary look made me very remorseful,' was Natalie's only rebuke.

Whatever the effort, Natalie kept the relationship alive, the contact real. She concealed disappointment, brushed off insult, and would not let many months go by without a meeting. But time showed up the limitations of their relationship. In February 1956, aged eighty, Natalie travelled to Nice and stayed at the Hôtel d'Angleterre so as not to encroach on Romaine's closed world. Each day they lunched together, but for the rest Natalie was banished so that Romaine could be alone with her dysfunctional muse. One afternoon Natalie walked by herself along the Promenade des Anglais: on a bench in the winter sunshine she struck up a conversation with a well-dressed, middle-aged stranger, Madame Lahovary. And so began a new affair.

23

We gathered for Ethylene's wedding in a marquee in her mother's garden. Pastor Serena wrapped her and Amy in a sort of blanket, sprinkled drops of oil on their bowed heads, blessed them, and prompted them to make their vows out loud. They said they would stay together, love and hold each other, and forsake all others until death did them part. They exchanged rings inscribed with their entwined initials.

Ethylene's mother looked bewildered, perhaps because of the absence of a man and men. She asked me what I was working on now, as she passed round the vol-au-vents.

29

Madame Lahovary

'I suppose we are slipping into old age.'

In May 1956 Natalie wrote ecstatically to Romaine from the Ritz in Madrid of the bracing air and the Goya paintings, of shopping for shoes and capes, and of a conservationist from the Prado who was cleaning frescoes with soap and Vaseline, and might clean Romaine's pictures too. Madame Lahovary just happened to be with her – 'because of motor trouble to her Studebaker'. Romaine replied with mournful news of constipation and failing sight, sad that the beautiful oleander on the upper terrace of her Fiesole garden had been destroyed by frost.

Blue-eyed Madame Lahovary had airs and graces, and was not in the mould of Natalie's previous lovers. She lacked fragility, and was undisturbed by either artistic ambition or a history of sexual adventure. She liked fashionable social gatherings, chiffon camellias on the sleeves of a blouse, low necklines, close-fitting feathered hats, a fur trim or gold brocade on a satin coat, and pearls on her slippers. Her conversation was domestic and her household organised. She was fifty-six – twenty years younger than her husband,

Nicholas, a retired Romanian ambassador; she had been his secretary before they married. Their joyless marriage was lived in moneyed comfort in an eighteenth-century house in Grandson, near Lake Neuchâtel in Switzerland.

Madame Lahovary knew of Liane de Pougy's beauty, of Rémy de Gourmont's *Lettres à l'Amazone*, and of Natalie's charisma and reputation, but there was nothing lesbian about her own lifestyle. Socially, she and her husband were at the fringe of the Proustian world of the Clermont-Tonnerres and the de Montesquious. She described her attraction to Natalie as a mental liberation and their relationship as a resurrection. Natalie, she said, gave her confidence and strength.

She was at pains, though, to conceal the nature of this relationship from her husband. She kept the semblance of marriage, so he tolerated, up to a point, Natalie ensconced for the summer in his house or in a nearby hotel, and his wife's frequent engagements in Paris. When he became suspicious and asked Natalie to leave his wife alone, she asked him to leave his wife alone, too.

Natalie seemed not to grow old in her mind or desires, though friends drifted into frailty and her sister Laura hobbled on canes and a frame. She stayed true to her creed of being true to herself, of being a poet of life. Alice B. Toklas, 'carrying on alone' in service to Gertrude, wrote to a friend: 'Natalie Barney has a new love affair. Isn't it wonderful? She's the one bright spot in a fairly cheerless world.'

In July, Natalie bathed in sulphurous waters at Yverdon for her rheumatism and circulation, and stayed at La Prairie, 'only five kilometres from my Lahovary friends where I am to lunch today'. She tried to entice Romaine to join her. 'I miss Nat Nat a lot, but nothing would get me to move for the present,' was Romaine's reply.

As it dawned on Romaine that Madame Lahovary was a significant force to Natalie, jealousy set in. 'I am glad you have found a nice Swiss friend,' she wrote to her on 13 October. 'But everyone wants to be your friend. The chief thing is to have real friends and not parasites.'

When the three of them met in Nice it was not a success. Romaine retreated to bed in a darkened room; Natalie, she said, seemed exhilarated and was showing off at her expense:

> I am not jealous, and only too glad to see you happy and occupied. But all this worldly life must take place apart from me
> . . . No brain can stand for long a continual bustle and movement which has nothing to do with it. The tittle tattle seems positively idiotic and I shall certainly keep away from it.

She said her happiest times were when she stayed in bed all day in Fiesole with cool air coming in from the garden through the wide-open windows: 'obliged to see no one, obliged to go nowhere'. Small things pleased her: a fine day, the jasmine bush in flower. In Nice she maintained her wartime paranoia about 'dark, murderous-looking creatures that roam around our Ponchettes quarters'. Her own sterility made her scornful of all artists: Goya was syphilitic; Braque unemotional and empty. When Natalie told her of Marie Laurencin's death in 1956, her uncharitable comment was: 'Men love silly women and their silly art tickles their vanity.'

Natalie, encouraging and reparative, asked Romaine to be forgiving, told her she loved the way she looked, her work, sensibility and strangeness, and that this other pragmatic love was less significant: 'I very much miss my bright angel's company, the only one I recognise for keeps. I never see or hear anything profound without feeling a homesickness at heart from not sharing it with you. We always respond alike. And so may it be as long as we last.'

They met at times and places conceded by Romaine, but Natalie now no longer discarded her own plans. Over a span of fifty years she had proved herself 'ever your loving and devoted Nat Nat'. She abided by Romaine's caprices, wishes, and commands and continued her acts of service, despite her own great age. She sent her pairs of black culottes, and Nancy Mitford's biography of Madame de Pompadour, recommended an ophthalmologist, and specialists for hernias and stomach upsets, sent details of reliable investment accounts, and sympathised with her angel's fury at being disturbed by a neighbour's barking dog. When Romaine's rented-out apartment in the rue Raynouard needed urgent repairs – the kitchen repainted, the sink and lavatories replaced – it was all for Natalie to organise. When it was judicious to sell the place because of tax problems with the undeclared rental income, she arranged it – and the auctioning of the Steinway, oak tables, armchairs, and eighteenth-century tapestries.

Madame Lahovary knew Romaine was central to Natalie and that she must not show resentment, or seek to rout her, if her own relationship was to succeed. She gave an open invitation for Romaine to join them at Grandson, and posted to her medicines for pains and lethargy. Natalie drafted a letter of thanks in French for Romaine to copy – she did not 'feel up to amiable phrases'.

To Romaine, Natalie described herself as quiet, well fed and often bored, though she wanted Madame Lahovary to be always with her. Gone were the evenings of her youth, 'bathed in moonlight and poetry'. As a point of honour she still made the most of life, 'as the leaves fall about my haunted garden and the best people are no longer there'. At a literary lunch she was intrigued to meet Isaak Dinesen who had just published *Seven Gothic Tales*.[1] 'She looks like a mummy with very living dark eyes. One can't abandon Paris altogether because of these frequent meetings with the valuable unknown.' She took melancholy walks with Laura in the gardens of the Bagatelle and they travelled together to Lausanne to the spas.

For Romaine, the wall separating her from the outside world became ever higher. 'What thoughts and occupations fill your days and evenings?' Natalie asked her with wonderment. The answer was not many. Romaine neither painted nor drew, and no visitor dared approach her. She seemed as weird as her mother, with the same confused feelings of hate. But behind her negativity there remained a vulnerability, a childlike unreasonableness and sense of hurt. Nothing in her formative years had shown her how to sustain social or emotional attachments, how to trust people or feel safe in their company. Natalie was the only person who ever got truly close to her, the only one who refused to be rebuffed. But even Natalie foundered against Romaine's intractable neurosis. It was there like a rock formation. With her love she hoped to erode it. She chipped at it, made no headway, then tried again.

---

1 Isaak Dinesen aka Karen Blixen (1885–1962). Born in Denmark at Rungstedlund, 25 km north of Copenhagen. When she was 10 her father killed himself. She married his cousin, Baron Boor von Blixen, and together they farmed in Africa. She contracted syphilis from him. Her best-known books are *Seven Gothic Tales*, *Out of Africa*, and *Winter's Tales*.

At times Romaine voiced the love Natalie knew she felt. 'As usual I miss Nat Nat very much,' she wrote, after seeing her on to the Paris train from Nice:

> in the dark comfortable car I was sad, and kept thinking about our long friendship which on my part is as great as ever: of our natures that differ fundamentally; you needing people as fuel for producing the sparks that animate your rare gift of rapid words and thoughts, and I needing solitude for creating art in my world of art. I cannot create in any direction without solitude. But we meet in so many other ways and what a joy it is when we do meet.

Romaine was caustic about Natalie's dependence on Madame Lahovary. On 15 July 1957, at the age of eighty-three, she wrote after a stay at Grandson that she had nothing in common with Natalie's friends; that one might view such people on the television, but then be glad to switch off and return to self and solitude. 'What really does matter is to find completely disinterested beings who live a little like oneself. When one misses this eventuality through others' fault, one's memories are not of the best. Please remember me to Monsieur and Madame Lahovary.'

She found no such disinterested beings. Only Natalie kept the lien of love alive. When Romaine journeyed to Paris, Natalie ensured that her room at the Continental, overlooking the Tuileries, was heated fifteen days in advance, that comfort of every sort was in place, and that no people were to be seen.

In December 1957, ensconced in the Hôtel d'Angleterre in Nice, Natalie dared to complain of the arrangement of being near

to Romaine, yet seldom seeing her. She was without Madame Lahovary whose husband – described by Natalie as 'fat and self-indul-
gent' – had suffered a serious heart attack. She saw her angel only
for unsatisfactory lunches, followed by long naps and curtailed
evenings. It was a pity, she said, that Romaine so put her own
comfort above all desire for their companionship.

Natalie brooked such disappointment and coped with her own
rheumatism and tricky heart. She was casual about publication in
America in 1960 of her memoirs of friends, *Souvenirs Indiscrets*,
saying she would have preferred success for Romaine's autobiography, and to see Romaine's paintings catalogued and housed in
galleries. 'Your gift is more straightforward and genuine,' she said
and meant it. She longed for Romaine, who in her turn longed
only for silence, and ate only watery things because she choked
on solids.

'I suppose,' Natalie wrote in July 1961, 'we are slipping into
old age.' Both took vitamins and pills for their digestions and their
hearts, and kept the heating on day and night. They feared the
loss of their money in another Wall Street crash. Natalie sent
Nabokov's *Lolita* and *Pale Fire* to Romaine, and Una Troubridge's
panegyric, *The Life and Death of Radclyffe Hall*. 'It's mostly about
dogs and nerves and John's end,' she said.

In June 1962, Monsieur Lahovary's problems with his heart esca-
lated. He could eat nothing, lost ten pounds' weight in a week,
and was admitted to a clinic in Lausanne. He died the following
month. Romaine sent words of sympathy to his widow. 'Will your
plans be changed?' she asked Natalie, anxiously. To which the
answer was yes.

24

You show me snapshots of your distant past: aged three with ringlets, in school uniform with wires on your teeth, on skis in Alpine snow, confetti raining on both you and a man I have yet to meet. You show me photos of your daughter. I search her face for a likeness to yours.

Good evening, ladies, the waiters say. I observe us in a glass, take those captured moments, and try to appraise where we now are. Transience is ever with us. I do not find it hard to love your lined eyes. You seem to believe me when I tell you what I once was like. The past is at most only a book. We have no option but to discard it. One thing or another will divide us. Will take us into the dark.

30

The Last Lap

'We are both still here.'

Natalie moved to the Grandson house after Monsieur Lahovary's death, and his wife became 'her Janine'. Natalie had endured two heart attacks, was short of breath, had problems walking and was unable to manage the stairs. There was pragmatism in choosing a relationship with a woman in sprightly middle age who had nursing experience and a comfortable, well-run, lakeside home.

Janine cared for her day and night. She was her nurse, travelling companion, secretary and lover. Natalie's hair was now white. There were no more extravagant displays. But she had saved Janine from 'the double defeat' of marriage, and inspired devotion in her. Natalie's reputation as the Amazon would continue to the grave.

'Which of all our pasts will be *the* Past?' Natalie had asked. Of them all, it was Romaine. But Romaine became by the day more solipsistic, less able even to acknowledge the existence of others. Her response to Natalie's news was cool. 'A love affair can cause trouble at our age, so do be careful.' She was, she said, relieved that Natalie was being taken care of, and then detailed at length how the opposite was true for her, what with smoking chimneys, smells and disturbances. She said perhaps she would go to Geneva and look for a house to buy where she would not be so isolated.

Natalie loved her as diligently, sympathised as deeply, was scathing about her 'monstrous mother' whom she was 'brave and wise enough to leave'. The experiences of early childhood stayed with them both, old though they were. Physically Natalie was weak. 'But I long towards my angel. Strangers come and go.' She wrote in a shaky hand, of dreading the months without Romaine, of wanting her letters. Romaine was her dearest and most cherished friend and companion, the person with whom she had most in common, with whom she felt entwined 'beyond the possibility of separa- tion. Even at night, each time I awake, you are my greatest preoc- cupation and greatest love.'

As ever, she let insult, accusation and rejection pass her by. She still worked to get Romaine's autobiography published and her pictures placed in galleries in France and the USA. She sent her vitamin B12 for her anaemia and calming pills for her nerves, advised treatment in Paris because of her failing strength and frequent falls, and worried about her haemorrhoids and constipa- tion. 'Janine suggests syrup of figs. I use it,' she wrote.

It distressed her that Romaine was isolated in her Villa Gaia, halfway up a hill without competent staff: 'You are far too delicate and rare a being to put up with all such trouble.' She suggested that Romaine close her house, leave it under police super- vision, and move to Grandson, 'where you can be well-fed and cared for under your Nat Nat's vigilant love'. At Grandson, she said, the chauffeur, valet, cuisinier, and femme de chambre were all excellent.

But Romaine was claimed by the 'nether world' of St Mar and her mother. What D'Annunzio had called her 'guarded sensitivity' became a prison. She suspected a 'maleficence' in her own servants, Gino and Anna, and believed they were stealing from her. She kept her autocratic standards: Gino wore a white jacket to serve her meagre supper.

In her Nice apartment she had locks and bolts put on all the doors, and she sold her paintings by Conder and Sargent so that they could not be stolen. In her studio was the portrait of Ida Rubinstein on a winged deathbed. Its silence filled her apartment. It was this silence, this vacuum, that she craved.

She achieved a kind of death within life: no people, no noise, no interruption. Her terrace in Fiesole was an earthly paradise of azaleas, geranium, and jasmine, all white. She wished Nat Nat could see it, but she wanted her in spirit, not body. 'I think of Nat Nat all the time. I am fighting old age and at times I fight well and then again I don't.' She had no strength. For half an hour she tried alone to get out of the bath, then rang for Anna: 'Fortunately the bell did not electrocute me and the door was not locked.' She spoke of grasping Anna's 'greasy neck' to be hauled out.

She went blind in one eye and could not see to read. Her doctor called regularly to treat her high blood pressure which Natalie said was caused by all the coffee she drank: Gino made it three times as strong as Berthe's. She fell three times in her garden because of weakness in her legs. 'Mine too are on the wane,' Natalie wrote. 'But my heart goes on beating and chiefly for my angel.' She was matter-of-fact about her own death but grieved at the thought of Romaine's. Romaine was resigned to dying. 'Find a brilliant aphorism for my state, darling. *Et n'en parlerons plus.*'

By contrast to Romaine's isolation, Natalie's was an indulged old age. The house at Grandson had an elevator, central heating and a driver available for all errands. Berthe came from Paris to teach Janine's cook Natalie's favourite recipes. And Janine was entirely devoted: if Natalie had a cold she put cologne on cotton wool for her to sniff.

In the summer of 1965, after much persuasion and palaver over maps, servants' rooms, garage arrangements and dietary needs, Romaine travelled to Grandson for a holiday. 'What a joy and welcome having you here,' wrote Natalie from her heart, but she annoyed Romaine by knocking on her door at least twice a day and the stay was not a success. The food was excellent, but the weather was poor. Romaine cried out each night in her sleep, and had terrible outbursts of rage. Janine said it was because she was a Taurean with horns beneath her brow. She advised an immediate blood test, in case Romaine broke blood vessels in her anger and ruined what was left of her sight.

The summer ended with Romaine vowing never to return. Natalie, ever positive, pointed out that despite no pleasant memories Romaine had achieved a great deal: she had seen good doctors about her health, and notaries about her will, visited Bryher whom she liked, and breathed the mountain air.

However bracing the air and comfortable the Grandson house, Paris was Natalie's home. In 1966 Janine moved with her to 20 rue Jacob and visits to Grandson became less frequent. 'And how is Janine who is no doubt with you?' asked Romaine, who was jealous. Aware that death was near for herself and her angel, Natalie worked to defy it. On her ninetieth birthday in October 1966 the *International Herald Tribune* ran a fulsome article about her verve, charm and original mind, her extraordinary salons and how central she was to the cultural life of the capital.

Many of Romaine's paintings had languished neglected in empty studios and needed restoration. Natalie arranged for portraits of Ida Rubinstein, Gluck, Carl Van Vechten and Muriel Draper[1] to be taken and restored by the Yale University Library. Twenty other of Romaine's paintings and her drawings, reviews, and cuttings, were taken by the National Collection of Fine Arts in Washington.

In spring 1968, Adelyn Breeskin,[2] Curator of Contemporary Art at the Smithsonian Institution, again at Natalie's instigation, visited Romaine in Nice to discuss an exhibition and the publication of a catalogue of her work. Romaine was ninety-four. She gave Breeskin lunch and tea and paid for her hotel, without her knowing. She asked for and received an assurance that her work would not be hung within sight of any by Alice Pike Barney. Adelyn Breeskin also said she wanted to publish *No Pleasant Memories* 'in handsome format' to show the triumph of art over devastating handicaps.[3]

Prompted by this interest, Romaine recorded a reading from the manuscript and sent a copy to Natalie who described it as wonderfully clear-voiced and interesting, though it lasted three hours. Natalie wrote of the pleasure of her Angel's voice coming to her as she lay in bed, the windows open to the second day of summer, the chirp of birds, the cuddling sound of doves, and 'my thoughts of you'.

---

1 Muriel Draper (1886–1952). American interior designer, society hostess, and writer of articles and sketches and of a memoir *Music at Midnight* (1929). She founded the Congress of American Women in 1949.

2 Adelyn Breeskin (1896–1986), an authority on the art of Mary Cassatt.

3 Publication did not happen.

That summer Romaine fell again, on a visit to her dentist in Nice. She did not want Natalie to get involved. But it troubled Natalie to think of her alone in bed in her darkened flat and she asked her to pack a case and to come to Paris. Édouard MacAvoy would collect her and her maid by car. Romaine refused.

Natalie sent constant notes of love: 'From Nat Nat's weak heart, full of love for her Angel.' 'Farewell to my Angel, as ever the nearest and dearest to my heart.' These notes went unacknowledged, though Natalie supposed they reached their home.

Disturbed by Romaine's silence, in December Natalie journeyed to Florence from Switzerland believing Romaine would not refuse to see her. But Romaine did refuse. She would not open the door. 'My angel and cruel love,' Natalie wrote. 'After half a century of being our nearest, why do you treat me like an unwelcome stranger?' She asked if she might call again the next day, just to be near, and to bring her own doctor to help. 'Do please I beg of you and our everlasting friendship, reassure me, or let me come to you. To hold your head on my shoulder and carry out whatever wish you may express to your ever loving and faithful friend, Natalie.'

But Romaine would not be consoled. It would be too much of an invasion or surrender in her final frailty to cope overtly with Natalie's love, to hear it spoken, or see it face to face. She aimed to go to the lonely death she chose.

'It is not the love I receive but the love I feel that matters,' Natalie had written when young. In the final year of Romaine's life she would not communicate with Natalie. Natalie's last surviving message, sent to her on 9 July 1969, read: 'My Angel is as ever first in my thoughts and deepest in my heart.' Romaine wrote on the envelope, 'Miss Barney. Paris.' And left it unanswered. All further letters she destroyed. She died alone in a darkened room on 7 December 1970. She seemed at her end to follow the same path as her mother: alone in yet another house, dependent on hired staff who gave paid service but no more. For fifty-five years Natalie had fought to keep Romaine in touch with 'the sunny outer world'. Romaine chose 'the negative exultation of those who are solitary and adrift'. If she was redeemed it was by her paintings and by the one staunch love she inspired. She made no effort to consolidate her reputation. When she died it did not matter to her that her exhibition catalogue was going to press.

By the terms of her grandfather's will most of her fortune went to the Goddard estate. Like her mother, she left boxes and trunks filled with miscellaneous possessions: old medicines, silk scarves, seventy identical berets, quantities of unworn clothes and unused paints, hundreds of gold coins stuffed into medicine bottles. Like her mother she lived as if in transit, on her way to a better place. She was buried in Menton beside St Mar, a proximity she would have detested. She provided her own epitaph: 'Here remains Romaine, who Romaine remains.'

For three months Janine kept news of this death from Natalie, whose response when she heard of it was calm. It was not Romaine's dying that grieved her, at the end of a long life, it was her turning away from love, her self-denial and waste.

'We do not touch life except with our hearts,' was Natalie's view. The years of living with Romaine during the war had been taxing, but she wanted them to continue. She feared Romaine's 'remorseless quality' but wanted her to be fond of her Nat Nat 'enduringly'. 'I belonged to everyone, she belonged to no one: we considered ourselves quite different, and yet in our loneliness we were alike.'

At the same time that Romaine was stonewalling her, Natalie lost her lease on 20 rue Jacob. A petition, signed by 300 people, was sent to the minister of cultural affairs to try to prevent the new landlord, Michel Debré, a minister of justice under de Gaulle, from ousting Natalie and reconstructing the house and temple. It pointed out how celebrated Natalie's salon had been and how intrinsic she was to the sixth arrondissement and to Paris.

The petition failed. Never one to dwell on what was lost, Natalie moved with Janine to a suite of rooms at the Hôtel Meurice with a view of the Tuileries. She gave away most of her possessions. 'There's nothing more to lose,' she said. She took a few things with her: the painting of herself as a happy prince, framed photographs of Romaine, Dolly and Renée. She wandered in her mind and was feeble in her body. Berthe became too ill to help, so Janine did everything: washed her, supervised her meals, arranged visitors.

The ardour and flamboyance of the *belle époque* had left only ghostly traces in this four-star hotel. Natalie's demise was a slipping out of life, not like Dolly or Renée, '*encore jeune, encore belle, encore avide*'.

Janine became the grande dame: heavily made up, dressed in gold lamé and a hat, with Natalie's jewels around her neck, including the 'river of mama', a cascade of diamonds that Alice Barney had enjoyed. 'Jewels are for young women,' Natalie said, perhaps remembering Liane, 'lit up by her jewellery like a city at night'. On Friday afternoons Janine invited guests – oil magnates and uprooted aristocrats – for cocktails and olives. They talked of cruises, dinners, and shows.

Janine had power of attorney over Natalie. For eighteen months she wrote the cheques and Natalie signed them. Berthe thought the sums spent 'unbelievable'. Natalie outlived Romaine by a year and died in Janine's arms on Wednesday, 1 February 1972.[4] She was ninety-six. Two days after her death she was buried near Renée Vivien in the cemetery at Passy. A photograph of Romaine was buried with her. About twenty people gathered for the last of her Fridays. One of them remarked that Natalie would not have chosen to be among them. 'She never went to a funeral in her life.'

It was love that Natalie affirmed, not death. 'I make you the splendid gift of the love you have for me,' she had written, for all her lovers, but especially for Romaine. And to herself she asked, and answered, 'What have you loved best? – Loving. And what if you had many choices? I would choose love many times.'

---

4 Janine was disappointed to receive only an annuity of fifteen-thousand dollars, and some of Natalie's paintings. Natalie's fortune went to her sister, Laura, and after both their deaths to charities. Janine returned to her Grandson house but died a year to the day after Natalie.

25

My own mother stayed sound in mind and body until she was one hundred and three. On Thanksgiving Day, Natalie's birthday, she left her unlit gas cooker on, went to bed and slept deeply, aided by ten milligrams of amitriptyline. After six hours the gas ignited. It seems it reached the unguarded flame of the pilot light on her central heating boiler.

I attended the second cremation and was moved by the excerpts from Schubert's piano sonata no. 19 (D960) with Wilhelm Kempff at the piano, and by Kathleen Ferrier's rendition of the aria from Gluck's Orfeo ed Euridice, *'What is Life to Me Without Thee'. My mother's death does not seem final and, like Natalie and Romaine, I stay true to the wonder of consanguinity in my waning years.*

SOURCES AND BOOKS

ABBREVIATIONS

AAA Archives of American Art, Smithsonian Institution, Washington DC

JD Bibliothèque Littéraire Jacques Doucet, Paris

McF McFarlin Library, University of Tulsa, Oklahoma

SIA Smithsonian Institution Archives, Washington DC

NMAA Alice Pike Barney papers, National Museum of American Art, Smithsonian Institution, Washington DC

The quips and quotes that start each chapter are mostly Natalie's. They are from her following works:

Chapters 1, 2, 14, 17, 19, 21, 23, 27, 28 *Éparpillements*, 1910

Chapters 9 and 24 *Lettres à une connue*, unpublished, 1899, JD

Chapter 3 'Samples from almost illegible notebooks' in *Natalie Clifford Barney: Selected Writings*, ed. Miron Grindea, 1963

Chapters 8 and 13 'My country tis of thee' in *Selected Writings*

Chapter 16 'On writing and writers' in *Selected Writings*

Chapter 28 'Short Novel' in *Selected Writings*

Chapters 4, 5 and 7 *Souvenirs Indiscrets*, 1960

Chapters 11, 15, 18 and 20 *Pensées d'une amazone*, 1920

Chapter 6 *Traits et Portraits*, 1963

Chapter 25 *The Woman Who Lives With Me*, privately printed, no date. See *A Perilous Advantage: the best of Natalie Clifford Barney*, translated by Anna Livia, 1992

BEFORE ROMAINE

1 Liane de Pougy
10 a poet and a madman

Liane de Pougy, *My Blue Notebooks*, translated by Diana Athill, 1979. And following

2 More Liane de Pougy
14 gave one the leisure

My Blue Notebooks

14 to be a poet

Souvenirs Indiscrets

15 I can't and won't

Natalie to her mother, 26 February 1895, Alice Pike Barney papers, AAA. And see Jean L. Kling, *Alice Pike Barney*, 1994

15 The first of all arts

More thoughts and half thoughts, *Selected Writings*

15 The water that I made shoot

Souvenirs Indiscrets. And following

16 Only those

Samples from almost illegible notebooks, *Selected Writings*

16 There are women

Éparpillements

17 I knew little of the demi-monde

Souvenirs Indiscrets

18 I already love your hair

Souvenirs Indiscrets

3 'Sonnets de Femmes'
20 passionate rebel

My Blue Notebooks. And following

21 God will punish you

Pensées d'une Amazone

21 Might I be the one

Éparpillements

21 Pierre Louÿs

Les Chansons de Bilitis, 1894

22 chaste and intellectual

Natalie Barney, *Memoires Secrets*, JD

23 Why try   *My Blue Notebooks*

23 One is unfaithful   *Éparpillements*

24 Yesterday I rode   Quoted in Jean Chalon, *Portrait of a Seductress, The World of Natalie Barney*, 1979

26 Ever since I remember   undated letter, c. 1900, Pike Barney letters, AAA

26 for those who never read them   Natalie Barney, *Quelques portraits – sonnets de femmes*, 1900

4 The Princess Ghika

30 stupefied by tenderness   *My Blue Notebooks*. And following

5 Lady Alice

33 I loathe the enthusiasm   *Pensées d'une Amazone*

34 Nothing aroused her   *Alice Pike Barney*

35 I had met Stanley   Stanley's 'Lady' Alice By One Who Knew, AAA, 1927

35 I fear that if   Richard Seymour Hall, *Stanley, An Adventurer Explored*, 1975. And following

39 Live and let live   Tribute to my Mother, Alice Pike Barney, 1953, AAA

39 His affection   *Souvenirs Indiscrets*. And following

6 Renée Vivien

43 If only I could live   Letters to Amédée Moullé 1894–5, Bibliothèque Nationale, Paris

44 Paris respects   *Souvenirs Indiscrets*

44 The moon sulked   *My Blue Notebooks*

45 Lay down those funeral flowers   Renée Vivien, *The Muse of the Violets*, 1977

45 In you I find   *Portrait of a Seductress*

46 was to make my life following   *Souvenirs Indiscrets*. And

46 For I would dance   Olive Custance, *Opals*, 1897

47 hoping to comfort   Philippe Jullian, 'Fresh Remembrance of Oscar Wilde,' *Vogue*, 1 November 1969

48 kissing the English   *Souvenirs Indiscrets*; Natalie Barney, poems to Olive Custance, the Berg Collection, New York Public Library

48 The moon slanted   *The Muse of the Violets* and *The Amazon and the Page*

7 More Renée Vivien

50 I took up my old social round   Douglas Murray, *Bosie: a biography of Lord Alfred Douglas*, 2000; George Wickes, *The Amazon of Letters*, 1977

51 the anguish   *The Amazon and the Page*; Renée Vivien, *A Woman Appeared to Me*; Colette, *The Pure and the Impure*, 1941

52 You are such   *The Amazon and the Page*

52 Renée is with   *My Blue Notebooks*

52 My heart beat following   *Souvenirs Indiscrets*. And

55 Let us forget   Natalie Clifford Barney, *Je me souviens . . .*, 1910

56 from a young   *Cinq petits dialogues grecs*, 1902

56 Her power like her fortune   *Portrait of a Seductress*

56 I have searched   *A Woman Appeared to Me*

57 harassed by   Natalie to Eva, c. 1907, JD

8 Renée Vivien's Death

59 To love what one has   *Éparpillements*

59 How could I know	Alfred Douglas, *Autobiography*, 1929
60 bending to	*Memoires Secrets*
60 Oh hands that I have loved	Eva to Natalie, c. 1907, JD
60 I tried in vain	*Souvenirs Indiscrets*
61 With her I dare not	*The Pure and the Impure.* And following

9 Rue Jacob

66 How wildly	Natalie Clifford Barney, 'On Meeting Death' from 'The Amazon of Letters, A World Tribute to NCB,' *Adam International Review*, vol. 29, no. 299
69 worthless boy pederast	NCB undated letter to her mother, AAA
69 What do I care	*Éparpillements*
70 I am a lesbian	*Éparpillements*
70 They say it is necessary	*Traits et Portraits*
70 At Miss Barney's	Sylvia Beach, *Shakespeare & Company*, 1956
71 I dread possessions	*Pensées d'une Amazone*
72 I didn't create a salon	*Portrait of a Seductress*
72 The universe came here	Edmond Jaloux, *Les Saisons littéraires* (1904–14), 1950

10 Rémy de Gourmont

Quotation by Rémy de Gourmont is taken from his *Letters to the Amazon*, translated and with an introduction by Richard Aldington, 1931

75 One should remain	*Letters to the Amazon*
76 like two children	Natalie Clifford Barney, *Adventures of the Mind*, translated with annotations by John Spalding Gatton, 1992
76 He climbed into	*Adventures*

BEFORE NATALIE

12 Ella Waterman Goddard

Much of the quotation in the chapters about Romaine is taken from her unpublished autobiography *No Pleasant Memories*, c. 1938, AAA. In the manuscript, each titled section is usually no more than a page. Quotation is made with the kind permission of the manuscript's owner, Richard J. Schaubeck.

See also, Meryle Secrest, *Between Me and Life: A Biography of Romaine Brooks*, 1976; Adelyn Breeskin, *Romaine Brooks: Thief of Souls*, 1971

92 She never failed	*No Pleasant Memories: My Mother*
92 no fixity	*NPM: Sadness*
92 She was quite gracious	*NPM*: *Mediums*
93 The atmosphere she created	*NPM*: *My Mother*
94 It was not long after	*NPM*: *Mediums*. And following

13 St Mar

97 a fanatic Long Lost	*NPM: St Amar*. And following
99 Looking back on this time	*NPM: Mrs Hickey*
101 Belonging to one parent	*NPM*: *The Visitor*
101 As I greeted	*NPM*: *I return to my Mother*. And following

14 The Artist

103 I was left there	*NPM: The Convent*
105 I fought hard	*NPM*: *The Riviera*
105 I still possess	*NPM*: *The Greek Girl*
106 photographic variations	*NPM*: *Mademoiselle Tobet*. And following

15 The Doctors

110 an occasional young gentleman	*NPM: Mademoiselle Tobet*
111 My dear Beatrice	AAA
112 The letter you sent	undated. Quoted in *NPM*
113 I knew nothing	*NPM:* *Rome*
114 hold the ancestral	*NPM*: *Mademoiselle Tobet*. And following

16 Rome and Capri
117 disgusting picture cards   *NPM: Rome.* And following
119 Among all the colony   E.F. Benson, *Final Edition*, 1940
121 Art for art's sake   Somerset Maugham, *The Summing Up*, 1938. And see Axel Munthe, *The Story of San Michele*, 1957; Compton Mackenzie, *My Life and Times*, 1965
122 Mr St Amar Goddard   *NPM: Return to Capri.* And following

17 More Ella Waterman Goddard
125 She knew that she was dying   *NPM: The Mortuary Chamber*
127 I fled through labyrinths   *NPM: Riviera Jungles*
128 It symbolised   *NPM: The Lay Figure*

18 John Ellingham Brooks
129 I knew that the monastic life   *NPM: Capri Again*
130 So there was to be no   *NPM: The Walking Tour.* And following
131 but as his work   *NPM: London*
132 Somewhere   *Final Edition*

19 Paris
138 She was distinctive   *NPM: Aunt Minnie*
138 I found myself   *NPM: Renée Vivien*
139 L'ésprit   NPM: *Une Reputation.* And see Michael de Cossart, *Food of Love: Princesse Edmond de Polignac and her salon*, 1978; *A Durable Fire: the letters of Duff and Diana Cooper*, ed. Artemis

140 on condition

Cooper, 1983
Food of Love

20 Gabriele D'Annunzio

144 But there before me

My Blue Notebooks. And see
John Woodhouse, *Gabriele
D'Annunzio*, 1998

144 To me, he represented

NPM: Gabriele D'Annunzio.
And following. And see Phillipe
Jullian, *Annunzio*, 1972; John
Wayne, 'Gabriele D'Annunzio:
Fire and Roses, Mountain, River
and Sky', 1997; Laura Claridge,
Tamara de Lempicka, 2000

144 past trials

NPM: Gabriele D'Annunzio

147 I felt you were unfortunate

Frances Winwar, *Wingless
Victory*, 1956. Quoted from
unpublished letters between
Romaine and D'Annunzio in
the archive of the Vittoriale.

21 Ida Rubinstein

151 I remember one cold

NPM: Ida Rubinstein. And see
Michael de Cossart, *Ida Rubin-
stein*, 1987; Ida Rubinstein,
'How I Came to Know D'An-
nunzio', *Novo Antologia*, 16
April 1927; Gerard Bauer, 'On
the Death of Ida Rubinstein', *Le
Figaro*, 17 October 1960

153 If it is considered

Quoted in Woodhouse, *Gabriele
D'Annunzio*

154 pouter pigeon

NPM: Natalie Barney

NATALIE AND ROMAINE

22 Natalie and Romaine

Six hundred letters between Natalie and Romaine, dating from 1924 to 1969, are in the archives of the McFarlin Library at the University of Tulsa, Oklahoma. They give insight into the nature of their lasting relationship. Quotation from Natalie's unpublished letters is made with the kind permission of François Chapon.

157 a real head and soul	'Romaine Brooks: The Case of a Great Painter of the Human Face', in *Adventures of the Mind*
157 I love my Angel	May 1927, McF
158 an unusual mind	23 Dec. 1921, Romaine to Radclyffe Hall. National Archives of Canada, Ottawa
158 gatherings of drunkards	20 May 1924, McF
158 wanting in all calm	16 May 1952, McF
159 Letters from Eva	quoted in *Portrait of a Seductress*
160 Was the Renault	Natalie to Romaine 21 July 1925, McF
160 and therein	25 July 1925, McF
160 Mrs Brooks puts bars	Elizabeth de Gramont, *Pomp and Circumstance*, 1929; *Years of Plenty*, 1931
160 So Renata Borgatti	21 July 1920, McF
162 Sick with anguish	quoted in *Natalie Clifford Barney: Selected Writings*
163 Don't thank Nat Nat	14 March 1953, McF

23 The Monocled Lady

165 You are going to tell	quoted in Jeffrey Weeks, *Sex, Politics and Society*, 1981
166 I am bold enough to say	ibid.
167 One always feels slightly	Radclyffe Hall to Eugenia

Souline, 6 September 1934, Harry Ransom Humanities Research Center, University of Texas

168 honeymoon — 20 May 1924, McF
168 I have been very lonely — 31 May 1924, McF
169 The elephant has come — Gluck, note on the back of a photograph of her painting of Romaine. The Fine Arts Society, London
170 It will live perhaps — 20 May 1924, McF
170 All these women — 5 June 1924, McF
170 When? Now? — 7 June 1924, McF

24 Dolly Wilde

172 more Oscar-like — Natalie Barney, *In Memory of Dorothy Ierne Wilde*, 1951
172 half androgyne — ibid.
173 Do you love me? — Dolly to Natalie, undated, JD. And see Joan Schenkar, *Truly Wilde: The Unsettling Story of Dolly Wilde*, 2000
173 On the street — *In Memory*
174 You have held — 23 July 1927, 14 July 1927, 28 July 1927, JD
175 These drawings — Quoted in *Romaine Brooks: 'Thief of Souls'*
176 messages which came — Édouard Macavoy, 'Romaine Brooks', *Bizarre*, March 1968
176 Your life at present — 18 February 1931, McF
177 I shall always serve — undated McF

25 More Dolly Wilde

179 beautiful, kind — *In Memory of Dorothy Ierne Wilde*
179 She is my Romaine — Dolly to Natalie, 28 July 1927, JD

180 that Romaine and Lily	Dolly to Natalie, 18 March 1932, JD
180 *The One Who is Legion*	A facsimile reprint was published by the National Poetry Foundation of the University of Maine in 1987
181 Paris is fatal to her	Natalie to Tancred Borenius, undated, JD
181 And we'll spend	Dolly to Natalie, 31 March 1934, JD
182 an uneducated	Romaine to Natalie, 7 December 1935, McF
182 Of course	Romaine to Natalie, 1 January 1936, McF
182 I shall remain	Natalie to Romaine, undated, McF
182 haggard and aged	Una Troubridge diary, March 1935, Harry Ransom Humanities
182 that *horrible*	Dolly to Romaine, 1935, JD
183 a slovenly impossible	Dolly to Natalie, 25 February 1939, JD
183 I am told	R. Toulouse to Natalie, 20 July 1939, JD

26 Ladies Almanack

191 so madly	See Barbara Guest, *Herself Defined: H.D. and Her World*, 1984
191 We neither of us	Robert McAlmon, *Being Geniuses Together: An Autobiography*, 1938
187 I was never a lesbian	see Hank O'Neal, *Life is painful, nasty and short . . . in my case it has only been nasty*, 1990; Phillip Herring, *Djuna:*

*The Life and Work of Djuna
Barnes*, 1995

27 A War Interlude

Quotation is taken from Romaine's unpublished autobiographical diary:
'A War Interlude or On the Hills of Florence During the War', AAA

197 Gertrude's staunch presence	Natalie's preface to Gertrude Stein, *As Fine as Melanctha*, 1954
204 I will need	Quoted in *Portrait of a Seductress*

28 Tenuous Freedoms

207 With the material	Janet Flanner, *Paris was Yesterday*
207 a nest of worries	Romaine to Natalie, 6 November 1946, McF
208 the mother of	Quoted in Suzanne Rodriguez, *Wild Heart: Natalie Clifford Barney's Journey from Victorian American to the Literary Salons of Paris*, 2002
208 precious life-giving	*Souvenirs Indiscrets*
208 I don't suppose	Natalie to Romaine, 1 March 1952, McF
209 No one is as busy	Natalie to Romaine, 15 January and 1 February 1952, McF
210 For me making	Romaine to Natalie, 22 September 1955, McF
210 Freud said	18 October 1955, McF
211 It would be a great	Max White to Natalie Barney, 29 November 1949, McF
211 My dead mother	*No Pleasant Memories*
211 I suppose an artist	24 May 1952
212 awful looking orientals	28 May 1952, McF
212 One must be careful	2 November 1955, McF

212 the mud, the dirt   ibid.
213 My angel's weary look   23 August 1955, McF

29 Madame Lahovary
216 because of motor trouble   12 May 1956, McF
217 Natalie Barney has   Alice B. Toklas to Mercedes de
                                         Acosta, 28 June 1956. Quoted
                                         in *Staying On Alone: Letters of
                                         Alice B. Toklas*, edited by
                                         Edward Burns, 1974
217 only five kilometres   9 July 1956, McF
217 I miss Nat Nat   12 August 1956, McF
218 I am not jealous   20 May 1957, McF
218 Men love   19 June 1956, McF
219 I very much miss   20 September 1959 and end of
                                         August 1958, McF
220 What thoughts and occupations   11 July 1957, McF
221 in the dark comfortable   10 May 1962, McF
222 Your gift   8 October 1960, McF
222 Will your plans   3 July 1963, McF

30 The Last Lap
224 Which of all   *Éparpillements*
224 A love affair   28 September 1963, McF
225 monstrous mother   24 August 1966, McF
225 beyond the possibility   8 May 1964, McF
225 Janine suggests   7 September 1966, McF
225 You are far too delicate   22 July 1966, McF
226 I think of Nat Nat   summer 1965, McF
226 Fortunately the bell   25 May 1966, McF
226 Mine too   3 November 1966, McF
226 Find a brilliant   7 September, 1967, McF
229 My angel and cruel love   Sunday morning 1968, McF
230 I belonged   *Thief of Souls*
232 I make you   *Éparpillements*. And following

More books

Allan, Tony, *Americans in Paris*, 1977

Burke, Carolyn, *Becoming Modern*, 1996

Cleyrergue, Berthe, *Berthe ou Un Demi-Siècle Auprès de l'Amazone*, 1980

Benstock, Shari, *Women of the Left Bank*, 1986

Carpenter, Humphrey, *Geniuses Together: American Writers in Paris in the 1920s*, 1987

Cody, Morrill, *The Women of Montparnasse*, 1984

Delarue-Mardrus, Lucie, *The Angel and the Perverts*, 1995

Fitch, Noel Riley, *Sylvia Beach and the Lost Generation*, 1983

—*Walks in Hemingway's Paris*, 1989

Field, Andrew, *The Life and Times of Djuna Barnes*, 1983

Ford, Hugh, *Published in Paris: American and British Writers, Printers, and Publishers in Paris, 1920–39*, 1980

Goujon, Jean-Paul, *Album Secret*, 1984

—*Renée Vivien*, 1986

Haight, Mary, *Walks in Gertrude Stein's Paris*, 1988

Hansen, Arlen, *Expatriate Paris: A Cultural and Literary Guide to Paris of the 1920s*, 1990

Jay, Karla, *The Amazon and the Page*, 1988

Klüver, Billy, and Martin, Julie, *Ki Ki's Paris: Artists and Lovers 1900–1930*, 1994

Lorenz, Paul, *Sappho 1900: Renée Vivien*, 1977

Morton, Brian, *Americans in Paris*, 1984

Palmer-Sikelianos, Eva, *Upward Panic*, 1993

Plimpton, George, *Truman Capote*, 1997

Putnam, Samuel, *Paris was Our Mistress*, 1947, 1987

Schenkar, Joan, *Truly Wilde*, 2000

Summerscale, Kate, *The Queen of Whale Cay*, 1998

Thurman, Judith, *Colette, Secrets of the Flesh*, 1999

Vivien, Renée, *A Woman Appeared to Me*, US edition, 1982

Weiss, Andrea, *Paris Was a Woman*, 1995

Wineapple, Brenda, *Genêt: A Biography of Janet Flanner*, 1989

List of Illustrations

Colour Plates

1 Romaine Brooks, Ida Rubinstein, in 1914 (oil on canvas 116 85 cm).

2 Romaine Brooks, *Self-portrait*, 1923 (oil on canvas, 118 68 cm).

3 Romaine Brooks, *Miss Natalie Barney, 'L'Amazone'*, 1920 (oil on canvas 86 65 cm).

4 Romaine Brooks, *Elisabeth de Gramont, Duchesse de Clermont-Tonnerre*, circa 1912 (oil on canvas 87 66 cm).

5 Romaine Brooks, *Gabriele D'Annunzio, the Poet in Exile*, 1912 (oil on canvas 118 91 cm).

6 Romaine Brooks, *The Crossing*, circa 1911 (oil on canvas 115 191 cm).

7 Romaine Brooks, *Renata Borgatti at the Piano*, circa 1920 (oil on canvas 142 189 cm).

8 Romaine Brooks, *Una, Lady Troubridge,* 1924 (oil on canvas 127 77 cm).

9 Romaine Brooks, *Peter, A Young English Girl*, 1923–4 (oil on canvas 92 62 cm).

10 Romaine Brooks, *La Baronne émile D'Erlanger*, 1924 (oil on canvas 106 86 cm).

11 Romaine Brooks, *Woman in a Black Hat*, 1907 (oil on canvas 163 114 cm).

12 Romaine Brooks, *The Huntress*, 1920. Also called *Decorative Portrait of Madame de Lamaire* (oil on canvas 130 97 cm).

PICTURE CREDITS

Numbers refer to the order in which the pictures appear.

Black and White Plates

Beaton Archive, Sotheby's: 12

The Beinecke Rare Book & Manuscript Library, Yale University Library: 13 © Man Ray Trust/ADAGP, Paris, + DACS, London 2004: 14

Bridgeman Art Library: 1, 2, 3, 4, 5, 6, 8, 10, 11

Smithsonian American Art Museum, Washington DC: 16, 17

Smithsonian Institution Archives, Washington DC (Alice Pike Barney Papers): 7, 18

Special Collections University of Maryland Libraries: 15

Colour Plates

Bridgeman Art Library: 3 (Musée de la Ville de Paris, Musée Carnavalet, Paris), 5 (Musée National d'Art Moderne, Centre Pompidou, Paris), 4 Mairie de Paris (Musée de la Ville de Paris) © 2004, Photo Smithsonian American Art Museum Washington DC/Art Resource/Scala Florence: 1, 2, 6, 7, 8, 9, 10, 11, 12

Acknowledgements

Text quotes are credited in Sources. My main research archive for unpublished material was the McFarlin Library at the University of Tulsa in Oklahoma where 633 unpublished letters between Natalie and Romaine are housed. The correspondence begins in 1920 and ends in 1969, a year before Romaine died. There are 271 letters from Romaine to Natalie and 362 from Natalie to Romaine. The main gap in the exchange is when they spent the war years together in Florence in Italy.

I drew too from Romaine's unpublished autobiography in the Archives of American Art at the Smithsonian Institution in Washington. Natalie's mother, Alice Pike Barney, aspired to make Washington the cultural capital of America. Her papers are also housed at the Smithsonian. They comprise an extensive archive of diaries, plays, photographs and an unpublished autobiography. I also found letters from Natalie and Renée Vivien in the Jacques Doucet collection in Paris. For obscure published works I used the British Library and the London Library.

For this reissue, and for his encouragement in commissioning my work, my thanks to Jon Riley at Quercus, the finest of editors. And thanks to Georgina Capel, my agent, who for fifteen years has shaped my career as a writer. And thanks, too, to Joshua Ireland at Quercus, who works on all aspects of publication and is unstinting in his efforts to get things right. I am lucky to have such support and encouragement. Team DS, Jon calls it. Thank you too to Charlotte Fry, John English, who proofread the new edition, and to Douglas Matthews who compiled the index. He excels at this complex art.

Index

Ace Bar, London, 19
Aivazovsky, Ivan: *The Tenth Wave* (painting), 148n
Albert, Prince of Wales (*later* King Edward VII), 13
Alexandre, Arsène, 141 & n
Alpine Gallery, London, 170
Anderson, Margaret, 84n
Anglesey, Mary, Marchioness of (*née* King; 'Minnie'), 47 & n, 138, 154
Anna (Romaine's servant), 226
Annunzio, Gabriel D': John Brooks reads, 130; commissions portrait from Romaine, 142; Liane de Pougy on, 143-4; relations with Romaine, 144-8, 152-3, 161, 203; at Arcachon, 145-6; and Donatella Goloubeff, 145-7; and Ida Rubinstein, 145-6, 152; debts, 148; Romaine satirises, 151; buys and furnishes house (Vittoriale), 153; elected President of Italian Academy, 153; in World War I, 153; sexual activities, 154; Luisa Casati's affair with, 161; reads Radclyffe Hall's *Well of Loneliness*, 166; death, 197; on Romaine's sensitivity, 226; *Francesca da Rimini*, 143; *The Martyrdom of Saint Sebastian*, 145-6, 150-2
Arcachon, France, 145-7, 176
Armstrong, Elizabeth, 133n

Bahai movement, 68 & n
Bakst, Leon, 145 & n, 154
Ballets Russes, 141n, 146
Balzac, Honoré de, 84n
Bankhead, Tallulah, 169 & n, 173n
Bar Harbor, Maine, 323
Barnes, Djuna, 3, 73, 167, 175, 187n, 191-3; *Ladies Almanack*, 3, 187-90, 192; *Nightwood*, 3, 192
Barney, Albert Clifford (Natalie's father):

and Natalie's prospective marriage, 14; Natalie's relations with, 15, 26; forbids Natalie to see Liane de Pougy, 24, 26; destroys Natalie's *Sonnets des Femmes*, 27; heart attacks, 28, 50; marriage, 36-9; background and career, 37; inheritance and wealth, 38; drinking, 39; illness and death in Monte Carlo, 53; Natalie takes ashes to New York, 54, 66
Barney, Alice (*née* Pike; Natalie's mother): studies art in Paris, 16; portrait of Whistler, 16n; with Natalie in France, 26, 44; criticises Natalie, 27; painting, 27, 44, 66, 158, 228; background, 33-6; inherits fortune, 33; relations with H.M. Stanley, 35-8; importance of money to, 36; travels, 36; marriage relations, 37-9; Natalie's fondness for, 40; portrayed in Colette novel, 51n; and husband's death, 53; cultural and social life in Washington, 66-9; Natalie meets in New York, 66; marries and divorces Christian Hemmick, 68-9; leaves USA for Paris, 69; at outbreak of Great War, 86; death and burial, 180-1; jewels, 231; *Jimmie* (play), 180; *The Woman* (play), 67
Barney, Laura (Natalie's sister) *see* Dreyfus, Laura
Barney, Natalie Clifford: casual lovers and liaisons, 1-4, 15-16, 44-8, 59, 62, 78, 136, 159, 182; character, 1; relationship with Romaine, 1-3, 157-63, 168, 195-6, 196, 207-10, 213, 218-19, 221, 224-5, 229, 232; Grecian Temple of Friendship, Paris, 2-4, 62, 69; life in Paris, 2, 212, 220; proclaims lesbianism, 4-5, 162; meeting and relationship with Liane de Pougy, 14, 16-18, 20-5, 323, 325; relations with